MY PESTLE IN MY HAND

Memories of a Pharmacist

MEDICINE AND MYTH

Presidential Address Given to the Worthing Archaeological Society

12th January 1954.

TRICK OF THE TRADE

A mystery on the Sussex South Downs

by

Frances Ann Roper

(née Hubbard)

Edited by

Judith Frances Hubbard

2018

In memory of Uncle Doc

With thanks to Nicolas George Hubbard
and
Penelope Phelps Forrest for their help

ISBN 978-1-5136-4007-5

9 781513 640075

Frances Ann Roper (née Hubbard)

b. 6 December 1899 (Chiswick)

d. 24 February 1985 (Worthing)

Photo taken December 1951

Introduction

Frances wrote this book in the early 1960's about her experience of pharmacy locums in hospitals in the 1950's. To retain the culture of those times, I have generally kept Frances's original wording. For instance, nowadays we talk about Psychiatric rather than Mental Hospitals.

As Frances says, she 'scrambled' names of people and places for the sake of anonymity. Some fifty or more years later I have taken the liberty, here and there, of revealing real names like Doc her husband. Doc was the nick-name of Major Arthur Cecil Roper (1890 - 1978) a keen archaeologist.

I have also named the hospital at Hemel Hempstead and the family connection locally through Sir John Evans KCB (1823 - 1908) of Nash Mills, an early patron and governor of that hospital.

Judith Frances Hubbard

August 2018

Foreword

This book is not written primarily for my fellow pharmacists, though I hope that some of them may find a bit of amusement in comparing their experiences with mine.

It is intended to give a glimpse of our life among the bottles to those who know little or nothing of our work. For this reason, I have deliberately avoided introducing anything in the way of "professionalism."

I have altered all names, if any name I have used fits any individual, I can only assure them that it is purely accidental. I have "scrambled" the incidents and descriptions in order to avoid making them too easily recognisable. Apart from "scrambling" everything is true to life.

Frances Ann Roper. M.P.S.

1960

The poem "The Apothecary" is reprinted by kind permission of PUNCH and subject to the consent of Sir Alan Herbert's Agents, Messrs. A.P. Watt & Son, to all of whom I extend my grateful thanks.

The poem has been my delight and inspiration since the days of my apprenticeship.

THE APOTHECARY

He looks respectable and mild,
Like someone at the Bar;
But then those bottles - Yes my child,
I do know what they are.

Those lovely globes of green and red,
They are not there for fun.
You see? He simply shakes his head;
He will not give you one.

But if the truth is what you want,
The trust is sweet and short,
For one of them is Creme de Menthe,
The other one is Port.

At even when he feels like sin
He takes them from the shelf,
And asks the naughty doctor in
And just enjoys himself.

He fills a bumper to the brim,
He lights a huge Havana,
And bawls the rude barbaric hymn
To Ipecacuanha.

The Song of Liquorice, the Song
Of Dr. Gregory's Powder;
The doctor sings both loud and strong,
The Chemist sings much louder.

At night they hold those hideous larks
And horrify the street
With pharmaceutical remarks
Which I must not repeat.

They drink the red, they drink the green,
Till they can drink no more,
Then drain a draught of neat quinine
And totter to the floor.

My son, the things you must not be
Compose a lengthy list.
But at the top I plainly see
The wicked pharmacist.
A.P.H.

By kind permission of Punch 1st March 1922

CHAPTER 1

Almost any book of reminiscences or autobiography written by a doctor, automatically becomes a Best Seller. Members of the Nursing profession are also highly popular in fiction and on radio and television. Doctors and Nurses are accredited with an aura of Romance, but what about us, the pharmacists?

No one ever looks upon us as figures of romance. We may - if the public ever thinks about us at all - be regarded as kindly, helpful entities in white coats, who will listen patiently to long recitals of the troubles of yourselves and your families unto the third and fourth generation, who will give you their close attention as you waste long minutes of their valuable time in choosing the exact shade of lipstick for yourself, or the precise colour and perfume of a cake of soap for Cousin Florrie, and who will show a perfect genius in remembering the type of food which is the one and only thing which your baby can be persuaded to take. Not forgetting to inquire tenderly about Granddad's rheumatics, or if Aunt Maud has got over her last "turn".

But Romance - No. In fact, we are hardly even considered as normal human beings. In hospital we are merely heads that pop through the hatch into the Out-Patients' Hall, call a name - which is invariably not yours, or so it seems to you - demand a shilling or its equivalent in stamp or ticket, hand out a bottle of medicine, box of tablets, jar of ointment or whatever, and promptly slam the hatch down again. And where is the Romance or popular appeal in that?

We have neither, the attractiveness of the nurses' uniform, nor the glamour of the doctors' stethoscope. Our white coats are usually more or less stained, and frequently frayed and torn. We are always in a hurry, always harassed and distraught, and our hands are usually grubby.

We are referred to indifferently as Chemist or Dispenser, and occasionally as Pharmacist. The public in general has not the slightest idea of any difference between these three states of being and couldn't care less. In point of fact, there is a very distinct difference. The term Chemist is a purely generic one and indicates anyone who is in any way connected with the study of chemistry. There are various types of chemist: - research, analytical and so on. We happen to be Pharmaceutical chemists. In popular parlance however, the word has become irrevocably attached to the obliging man in the shop around the corner, where you buy your cosmetics, toiletries, aspirin and baby food, and where you go to be weighed when on a diet.

It is required by the Law of the Land that on any premises where dispensing is undertaken there should be at least one person who is a Pharmacist. A Pharmacist is one who has been through the long and exacting course of study and training laid down by the Pharmaceutical Society, and who holds the Society's qualification. This course of training is almost as long and fully as exacting as that of a doctor and carries with it the responsibility of handling all poisons. The pass-marks in the qualifying examination are the highest in any profession, and many aspirants fall by the wayside, or only achieve the qualification after numerous heart-breaking attempts. This high standard is absolutely essential as we, the qualified pharmacists, literally hold the power of life and death in our hands.

On one occasion in hospital, I, in my favourite role of interested onlooker, was listening to a discussion between the chief Physiotherapist and the chief

Radiographer. These two ladies were trying to ascertain which of their respective jobs was the more responsible with regard to the welfare and safety of the patient. The discussion very soon deteriorated into an argument, which rapidly became more and more heated and acrimonious. I enjoy a good discussion, but arguments bore me, and the more heated they become the more bored I get. I took no part whatever, but when the fur as last began to fly in earnest, I remarked very quietly "If you are trying to decide who can do the most damage to the patient in the shortest possible time, just remember that in my job I can kill more people in five minutes than you could together in five years."

They both stopped dead and stared at me, then admitted that I was right, and neither had another word to say. It was probably very nasty of me, but I take an immense pride in my profession, in its vast antiquity and tremendous traditions, with which no other profession except that of the Physician, as distinct from the Surgeon, can compare.

Dispensers are people who have very good knowledge of the actual compounding and dispensing of medicines, but who have not passed the qualifying examination of the Pharmaceutical Society. I have found almost invariably that they are excellent at their work, competent and conscientious, and quite frequently more efficient than some Pharmacists. Many of them have passed the examination of the Apothecaries' Society, which is a far older foundation than the Pharmaceutical Society, but they are not allowed by law, to handle poisons except in the presence, and under the supervision of either a doctor or a pharmacist. Pharmacy is so closely bound up with the Law of the Land and so tightly restricted by the Dangerous Drugs Act, which comprise the brain-racking subject known as Forensic Medicine, that, for the protection of the public, and to keep a rigid check on the horrors of drug addition, only doctors and pharmacists are allowed to keep or handle a certain set of drugs.

When acting as Chief pharmacist at a certain hospital which is in two separate buildings one at each end of the town, I have often walked along crowded streets, jostled by mobs of shoppers, carrying in my innocuous-looking hand bag, a quantity of drugs which, if they had fallen into the right (or wrong) hands would have set me up for life with a yacht on the Riviera and a villa in Capri.

I have done my fair share of work in retail, that is, in chemists' shops, but ever since my apprenticeship days I have never liked it. To me it has always seemed completely wrong that pharmacists who have been through that long training and to whom is committed such great responsibility, should spend so much of their working life in selling toothpaste and nail brushes. Granted, they also do a great deal of dispensing, but to my mind the profession should never have been allowed to amalgamate with the shop-keeping. In Holland and many other countries there are no chemists' shops as we know them in England. There is a Pharmacy in each area, calculated on percentage of population, and in these establishments nothing but pure pharmacy is practised. All prescriptions are taken there to be dispensed, and nothing in the way of toiletries or cosmetics is sold. These can be obtained at any of the many shops which specialise in them, such as we should call drug stores in England, but in this type of shop no dispensing is done and no drugs are kept. In this way pharmacy is given its true status as a profession, and pharmacists are as highly respected as doctors.

Originally, I had hoped to be a doctor, like my father and both grandfathers before me. My mother and many of her numerous brothers and sisters were in the medical world, and I have always maintained that I was born with more drugs than blood in my veins. However, my father, knowing only too well the strain of a doctor's life, and knowing also that I had not the physical strength or stamina to stand up to it, decided otherwise. Nursing never appealed to me, so pharmacy it was.

I qualified between the wars, at a time when the prospects in pharmacy were at a very low ebb. Hospital posts, the work I longed for, were almost at a premium, and there remained only retail, or private dispensing for a doctor. Jobs in private practice carried very small salaries and no prospects, and in retail the salaries were equally poor, the hours scandalous, and the conditions incredible. I started my training full of enthusiasm and high hopes, and my college career was one of the happiest times of my life. I loved every minute of it, and my brain absorbed everything like a sponge. After the triumph of the final exam came the heart-breaking disillusionment. It was retail or nothing. I chose the latter. Fortunately, I was in the position of not being financially obliged to work for my living, and in anger and bitter disappointment I turned my back on pharmacy - as I thought - for ever.

I did this and that for several years, then married, and continued to do this and that including a considerable amount of globe-trotting with my husband. Then came the Second World War. We packed up our home and both leapt into uniform. I had so completely abandoned any thought of pharmacy that it never occurred to me that I might take it up again as a reserved occupation. I had, I thought, entirely eschewed Aesculapius and everything that was his; but in spite of myself I could never forget him. Every time I entered, or even passed, a chemist's shop during all those years, I would find myself looking wistfully at the ranks of bottles and sniffing the pungent air like an old war horse sniffing the battle.

Mars, whom I had hoped to serve, would have none of me. After a very short time in the A.T.S. my health broke down, and I was discharged on medical grounds as unfit for further service. Whereupon Aesculapius put forth his hand and made one grab, and before I knew what was happening, I was back in pharmacy again.

My knowledge had grown so rusty over the years, that at first, I could hardly distinguish a drachma from a scruple, but by dint of much puffing and blowing, and thanks to the help and unfailing patience of a pharmacist friend, whose flat I shared for a time over her shop, it all came back. Until the end of the war I was working steadily both in retail and hospital, and happier than for a very long time.

A month or so after the end of the war my health let me down again. This time it is good-bye Aesculapius the Roman god of healing and medicine for ever, I thought, and forthwith plunged into Good Works. Never was such a Good Worker and assiduous Committee-Sitter. I became Secretary of this, Chairman of that, President of something else, and plain Committee Member of several others. Doc was released from the Army and came home to a nine-to-five job and a wife who was racing round like a car engine out of gear and with a jammed accelerator. And getting nowhere fast.

The Health Service came in, bringing with it the greatest and most far reaching alterations and re-adjustments which have ever affected the Medical world in an equally short space of time. Beyond registering our names with the doctor who had looked after us for years, I regarded the whole set-up with complete detachment and a somewhat jaundiced eye and scuttled off to a few more Committee meetings.

Then out of the blue, Aesculapius sounded his last and most imperative summons. It was so utterly unexpected, so completely outside my scheme of things, so entirely at variance with the busy life I had built up for myself, that it left me shaken and incredulous. Surely it could not be possible that I should go back to pharmacy again. There could be no place for me in the world of modern medicine; I was years older than I had been when I went back during the war; I was over fifty, a back number. I knew enough to realise that enormous strides had been made in the discovery of new drugs since the war, but beyond that I had not the remotest idea of the changes and developments which had come about in the train of the Health Service.

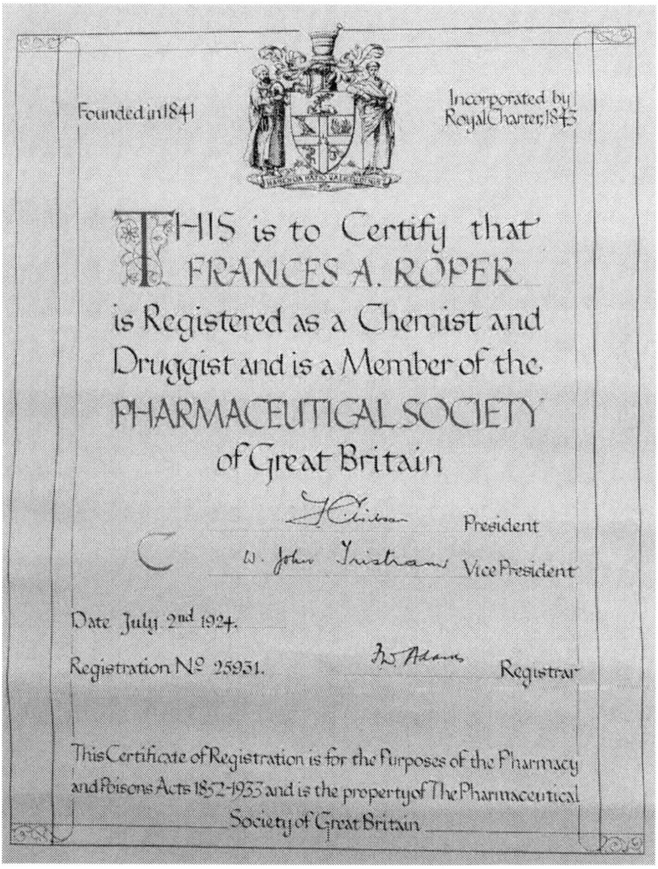
Founded in 1841

Incorporated by Royal Charter, 1843

THIS is to Certify that FRANCES A. ROPER is Registered as a Chemist and Druggist and is a Member of the PHARMACEUTICAL SOCIETY of Great Britain

President

Vice President

Date July 2nd 1924.

Registration No 25951.

Registrar

This Certificate of Registration is for the Purposes of the Pharmacy and Poisons Acts 1852-1933 and is the property of The Pharmaceutical Society of Great Britain

Frances was twenty-four years old when she qualified in 1924.
This certificate, which uses her married name, replaces the original.

CHAPTER 2

After a period of rehabilitation under Doc's kindly eye, I took various more or less long-term posts both in retail and hospital, around my own home area, till at last I felt myself competent to undertake the work at which I was aiming. This was to become a full-time locum, so to speak. The columns of advertisements in the Society's Journal every week, convinced me that there was more than enough demand for locums in hospitals alone, let alone in retail, to keep me fully occupied for as many months of each year as I wished to work.

I have never liked to commit myself to a permanent job. There is a strain in my family which suffers acutely from the condition known as ants in the pants, and I am one who has inherited it. Committing ourselves to a permanent job induces a suffocating sense of claustrophobia, and if, by a stern sense of duty, we try too hard to conquer it, a nervous breakdown in the inevitable result. We can work at top pressure and enjoy it thoroughly, as long as there is a date-line ahead, and the prospect of moving on elsewhere. It is not a particularly enviable characteristic, but it is so much part of our make-up that it is quite impossible to do anything about it.

The demand for locums was the complete answer for me. By undertaking locum work I could be sure of staying in any given post for not more than a few weeks at a time, I could arrange my own bookings and choose my own jobs. If I found the post uncongenial I could quite well put up with it for a week or so, and if I liked it, and were asked to go again, I should always be glad to do so.

Up till this time I had never been in charge of a hospital pharmacy, either as Acting Chief, or single-handed. All my hospital experience had been in the capacity of Assistant. Also, I had never lived in a hospital. During the war I had lived in digs, and otherwise had worked near enough to my home to be able to go to work from there every day.

Now at last I felt ready to launch out. Doc was in full accord with my plans and gave me every encouragement. He is an extremely competent and independent person, having been born and brought up in the back woods of Tasmania. He is a far better cook than I am, loathes being waited on, and takes the ups and downs of a house in his stride. He was extremely pleased when I got back to my job in pharmacy and has often remarked that since doing so I am far better tempered and pleasanter to live with, than I was during the years when I was trying desperately to be a good housewife.

Together we scrutinised the advertisements for locums, and at last settled on one which looked very attractive for my first venture away from home. It was a single-handed post in Devon. Immediately I visualised a quiet little country establishment of the Cottage Hospital type. It would have not more than twenty-five to thirty beds, and being advertised as single-handed, the work would be very light. With great excitement I wrote, asking for particulars. Within a few days came the answer; - it was a Mental hospital with between 800 and 900 patients!

This information knocked me completely sideways. My first reaction was a definite NO, very loud and clear. In common with a vast number of people, I had not the remotest idea of what a mental hospital was like, or of conditions under modern methods. I had awful visions of innumerable locks, bolts and iron railings, of padded cells whence issued horrible maniac screams, of tough warders strapping violent lunatics into straight jackets, and of an overall atmosphere heavy with depression and madness. Also, there was the alarming fact that I should be expected to cope single-handed, with the dispensing for close to 900 patients. In a General Hospital a hundred or so is about the limit when single-handed.

Doc was as shaken as I was, and we spent the evening between bouts of agitated discussion, and long deadly silences, both immersed in thought. Eventually the ants in my pants got the better of me.

"If it is a single-handed job," I said, "it means that somebody is doing it single-handed, and if they can do it, why can't I?"

Doc agreed to this flight of logic.

"Also", I went on, "it can't be actually dangerous, or they wouldn't advertise it calmly like this. If other people can work safely in a mental hospital, why can't I?"

Once again Doc agreed.

"There can't be any actual danger," he said, "they must have the patients under control, and it would certainly be an experience for you. Why not have a bash at it?"

This put it in the light of a "dare", and never since my nursery days could I resist a dare.

"Up girls, and at 'em," I exclaimed, and in this frame of mind I wrote back confirming the engagement.

Accommodation was to be provided in the Nurses' Home, and I should have a reliable cadet and porter to help me in the pharmacy. I have never encountered cadets in hospital work, and had not the slightest idea what to expect, but I did know that a pharmacy porter could either make or break the pharmacist.

Pharmacy porters are a breed unto themselves. Almost invariably they are superbly reliable, competent and highly intelligent; the very nature of their work requires that they should be. The first thing I do whenever I go to a new hospital is to make friends with the pharmacy porter and get help and support. I play shamelessly upon their innate chivalry, and by appealing to them as fellow human beings I have never yet had one of them let me down. A smile, please and thank you, a brisk bit of back chat in the middle of a rush of work, a cheery greeting first thing in the morning, and, however tired we all may be in the evening, a quick "cheerio, see you in the morning," and they will work themselves to a standstill for you. Above everything I try to avoid giving direct orders. It takes no extra time to say - please could you find me this or that, or - would you please fetch me another winchester of Paraf: Liq: and to say thank you when the required object is placed by your hand, and it pays dividends over and over again. I am proud to think of the dozens of Harrys, Jims, Charlies, Joes, Johns, Bobs, and even a beloved Benjie, whom I can count among my firmest friends. Some are quick, some are slow, some are golden-hearted rough diamonds, and some have the gentle polished manners learnt in their younger days when they were valets and butlers.

Many are ex-Petty Officers and N.C.Os. but whatever their background, never has any one of them used strong language in my hearing or behaved towards me as anything but a true gentleman. I love them all dearly and say from the bottom of my heart "God bless them all".

When my friends learned that I was going to work in a mental hospital their reactions were quite startling. Most of them gave me the impression that I was qualifying as a patient, and that horrible phrase "loony bin" was freely bandied about. I am ashamed to admit now that I used it myself, and at that time considered it highly amusing. As the time approached I began to feel like Daniel preparing voluntarily to enter the lions' den. On the one hand I hated leaving Doc and my comfortable home, while on the other hand there was all the excitement of the unknown. The anticipation of possible danger added a terrific kick.

It had been arranged that the hospital coach should meet me at Plymouth, but when I arrived after a very long journey, tired with travelling and over-excitement, no coach was there. I learned later that the directions to the driver to call for me at the station had been overlooked, and I was offered most dismayed apologies. I waited and waited, unwilling to engage a taxi, as I knew the hospital was about eleven or twelve miles away, on the slopes of Dartmoor. The porters at the station were most concerned on my behalf. They all knew the hospital coach well, and its usual times for coming to Plymouth, and when I suggested phoning the hospital they told me that the time of the coach's last visit to town was long past, and that I should have a very long wait if it were to be sent in on purpose for me. It was already very late, so I took a taxi.

After a long distance on the main road we suddenly swung sharply to the left, up and incredibly steep lane, and the driver told me we were nearly there. A little further on he pointed out some buildings half hidden among trees in a fold of the moors, under a huge escarpment which climbed high into the sky beyond. I stared in amazement. Where were the forbidding walls, the tall over-curved iron railings and barbed wire enclosures I had expected? The wayside hedges merged imperceptibly into banks of rhododendrons, veronica and hydrangea, then a drive appeared, wider and better surfaced than the lane itself, with a modest notice board showing the name of the hospital. We passed the entrance to the drive which swung steeply uphill between high banks and hedges, but where were the great iron gates?

There were no gates, iron or otherwise, just a wide, friendly drive flanked by towering masses of flowering shrubs and tall trees. My amazement grew and grew.

A few yards beyond the entrance to the main drive the taxi stopped before a large handsome building, standing a little way back from the lane, behind hedges and lawns. There were light wrought iron gates here, which were closed in a perfunctory sort of way, but their object was mainly to restrict the activities of an extremely lively Pekinese, who was chasing nothing in particular with great energy all over the lawn. I regarded him with the utmost delight. I am not fond of dogs in general, but am a complete and abject Pekinese fan, and this little fellow was almost the exact double of a beloved gentleman who had ruled our home and lives years ago. As I came to the gates he rushed up, barking madly, but there was no animosity in his bark. His job was to bark at strangers, and he was merely doing his job. We very soon became the best of friends.

CHAPTER 3

The revolutionary changes in mental hospitals and in the treatment of mental patients have only been made possible by the discovery of the new drugs. My first experience of mental work was in 1955, and, though I did not realise it at this time, it followed very closely upon the introduction of these true wonder-drugs. Until that time almost the only type of medicament which could be used for controlling patients was either paraldehyde or chloral hydrate. These have been known and used for many years, in fact ever since the old Asylums were originally built. They are still in use, and each is quite invaluable in its own sphere, but though they have the effect of keeping the patients fairly quiet and making them sleep, they have none of the therapeutic effect of the new drugs.

It is entirely due to the new drugs that walls and iron railings have been removed, that padded cells and strait jackets have gone out of use, and that boys and girls in their 'teens can safely and fearlessly tend and move amongst crowds of patients who, only a few years ago, would have been violent and dangerous. As well as the new drugs, there are also the new methods of various kinds of shock treatment, and techniques of brain operations which have effects which can only be described as miraculous, but the basis of the treatments is always the drugs.

I learned a great deal about the changes in mental hospital life from an elderly male nurse at the hospital in Devonshire. This hospital is, as I have said, one of the most progressive in the country; it was one of the first to use the new drugs and to introduce the alterations and improvements which their use makes possible.

Working at the bench one day, I heard a step behind me, and looking round saw a huge, burly man in the uniform of a Charge Nurse, smiling down at me. Another unusual feature of this hospital is the fact that the pharmacy door is never closed during working hours, and staff and patients alike roam in and out in the friendliest fashion. Of course, the pharmacy is never left open unattended, but otherwise it is always open, and when once or twice I have closed the door for protection against the howling draughts which rage down the corridors at times, great dismay has been registered by all. Having to knock for admission, which is the usual thing in most other hospitals, is regarded here as quite an insult.

My new friend had ex-policeman written all over him, and that, in fact, he was. He had been there close on thirty years and was due to retire in a few months' time. I asked him to tell me something of the changes he had seen in that time.

"You wouldn't know it for the same place now," he said, "everywhere was locked and bolted like a prison. There are twelve padded cells on the male side and twelve on the female, and up to the last year or so every one of them was in constant use. Now there is only one on each side, and they are very seldom used; all the others have been made over into private rooms. Strait jackets? We were always having to strap patients into them and strap them down on their beds to save them from flinging about and hurting themselves. But they haven't been used for a long time. In fact, I came across a whole pile of them stacked down in the cellars, covered with cobwebs and just rotting away. They are just a joke now, same as the padded cells. If one of the patients gets a bit uppish we tell them we'll put 'em in the pads, and they laugh their heads off. Some of them really like a spell in the pads, they say it's nice and quiet, and they can be on their own for a bit.

"The male nurses were nearly all recruited from the police force," he went on, "we had to be. Big strong chaps were needed, and especially those who knew how to catch hold of people without hurting them. I've played in the staff football team here till I got past it, and I've been manager ever since. For most of my time here we never had any trouble in raising a good heavy side from among the male nursing staff, but this last year or so it has been a real headache finding any fellows to play. They are all slim young lads now. They can manage the patients as well, and better, than us big heavy chaps, but they are not good for raising a football team."

The new drugs make the patients far more gentle and docile, without actually making them drowsy, and on the basis of this new docility is built the tremendous organisation known as Occupational Therapy. This is often considered to mean learning to make felt rabbits and woolly rugs, but there is far more to it than mere handicrafts, though these play a very important part. It means finding carefully graded occupation for every single patient who is capable of doing anything at all. By giving each one the work they can do, and enjoy doing, the results are staggering. Interest is gradually stimulated, self-respect is re-born, and even the most withdrawn and apparently hopeless cases can be restored to a great measure of normality.

It is much easier to find occupation for the women patients than for the men. Women patients have usually had their own homes and are only too happy to be given easy work in the sewing rooms, the laundry, the kitchens, or as cleaners and at household jobs. These come naturally to them, and they are all paid a weekly wage for the hours of work done. This they can spend in the hospital shop or save to spend outside when they go home for a few days leave.

The male patients are employed, according to their capacities, on the hospital farm, in the nursery and flower gardens, in the bake-house or shoemakers' establishment, as well as being taught trades and hand crafts.

Will, my kindly loveable Will, of the huge hands and the broad slow speech, had been a male nurse in the bad old days of not so long ago.

He could tell terrible tales of how, when a male patient became violent, half a dozen male nurses would be told to fight with him and reduce him to some sort of manageability by sheer exhaustion, before the doctor could approach him to administer any sedative. But Will hated the mere memory of those days, and I had worked with him on many visits before I even learned that he had ever been a male nurse. The word "violent" is never used now. However much that condition may be meant, the word "disturbed" is invariably used. This is all part of the new approach to mental sickness, with its all-pervading emphasis on kindness and understanding.

The great majority of patients were allowed complete freedom to wander about the park and grounds, and I found it very difficult at first to distinguish patients from staff, when the latter were out of uniform. It was only when some quiet and apparently entirely sane and normal person came out with some surprising remark, that I realised the position. The patients were everywhere, strolling in the grounds, sitting on the seats alongside the drive, and frequently dropping in to the pharmacy for a chat.

On my way up to the main drive one morning, I nodded a greeting to a quiet, pleasant-faced woman on one of the seats. She returned my greeting with a smile, then said, "You're Lady Mountbatten, aren't you?"

I was still too new to the life not to be somewhat shaken, though I did at least know that it is always better to humour the patients rather than contradict them and upset them unnecessarily. However, I could hardly have unmerited honour thrust upon me in this way. I have never seen Lady Mountbatten except in photographs, though I imagine there may be a slight general resemblance in slimness and fairness.

"No, dear," I said, after a moment's brisk thinking, "I am not Lady Mountbatten". I felt quite apologetic at disappointing her. She scrutinised me severely. "Well, you're very much like her," she said obviously thinking I was lying. I felt more apologetic than ever. "Anyway", she went on more cheerfully, after eyeing me carefully for a minute, "I expect you're one of her retinue". I did not feel capable of entering into any more discussion but left it at that and fled.

Another time a neatly dressed elderly man came into the pharmacy and stood looking round at the shelves and apparatus. He might have been a highly respectable commercial traveller. I hadn't a clue as to who he was, but said good morning politely, and asked if I could do anything for him.

"I just came in to have a look round," he replied, "I used to be in this line myself". I was all prepared to welcome a brother pharmacist when he went on, "but they're teaching me carpentry now." The penny dropped, and I realised he was a patient. We had a friendly and perfectly normal chat, except for the ever-recurring refrain, "But they're teaching me carpentry now."

Another elderly, well-dressed man came in one day. We had a long chat about things in general, and there was not a sign or a hint that he was anything but completely sane and normal. After we had become on thoroughly friendly terms, he said, in the same perfectly ordinary voice. "I had a visitor last night." I was mildly surprised that visitors should be allowed in at night, but merely said, "Oh, who was that?" "I don't know who it was," he replied. "It was a very young man and he was all shining white from head to foot. Very beautiful he was." "What did you do?" I asked. "Did he speak to you?" "No", he answered, as if it were the most ordinary thing in the world to see an angel at his bedside, "he came and stood by my bed for a bit, and it made me feel much better to have him there. Nobody else in the ward saw him, but I wasn't frightened, and presently he went away".

This conversation made a deep impression on me. I believe in the existence of angels as completely as I believe in the existence of my fellow human beings, and I could see no reason whatever to doubt but that this man had actually seen one. When one part of the human mentality is clouded or out of gear, other perceptions are set free to develop, in the same way as a blind person develops power and sensitivities which are present in every human being, though atrophied through lack of use.

When the regulations and rates of salaries were being fixed under the Health Service, they were based on the conditions prevailing at the time. Mental hospital pharmacists were placed in a far lower category than general hospitals, salaries were lower, and in every way the mental hospital pharmacist was treated as a very inferior being.

Within the last five or six years the picture has changed rapidly and fundamentally, as much in the pharmacy, perhaps more than in the other departments. The work is now fully as heavy as in a General hospital. In many ways it is far more exacting, as new drugs and preparations are coming out every other week, and the treatments of the individual patients are constantly under revision. Yet the status and salaries are still what they were in 1948.

Many mental hospital pharmacists with whom I work and for whom I undertake locum duty are middle-aged men who have been in the same hospital for anything from fifteen to more than thirty years. The sudden pressure of heavy work being put upon them after so many years of an easy and quiet job comes as a great strain. During those easy years many of them undertook all sorts and kinds of extra jobs in the hospital, with the result that I, coming in as a locum, find myself expected to undertake at a moment's notice, any and every sort of work, much of it entirely unconnected with pharmacy. The demands range from mending broken spectacles, taking charge of and issuing all the Theatre instruments, coping with broken sphygmomanometers and laryngoscopes, dealing with all the gas cylinders (though they often come under the pharmacist's charge in general work) to running the cricket and football sweeps, and dealing with dead mice. No, the life of a full-time locum is not an easy one; but on the other hand there is never a dull moment, and it keeps me on my toes till I am nearly air-borne at times.

All these extraneous jobs are in addition to the everyday work of ward baskets and patients' prescriptions. There is one blessing in mental work - it is only very rarely that one has Out Patients to deal with. The vast majority of patients are resident, and it is only at very specialised hospitals such as The Maudsley, (The Maudsley Hospital is a British mental institute in south London. The Maudsley is the largest mental health training institution in the UK.) that there are Out Patients clinics. The idea of Out Patients in mental work is creeping in, however, for among the most recent developments in the treatment of mental illnesses is the discovery that numbers of sufferers respond to treatment far better if they can live in their own homes, and be with their own people, coming to the hospital every so often for treatment and fresh issue of tablets rather than be segregated entirely from normal life as In Patients.

The whole vast field of mental work is going through an upheaval and reorganisation such as has never been known before. I find it so fascinatingly interesting that this last year or two I have practically given up General work and am devoting my time more and more to Mental. I was discussing the subject with the Deputy Matron of a very progressing mental hospital recently. She put the whole thing in a nut shell.

"I prefer mental work to general," she said, "just as you do. I feel that in general work everything has got to such a high pitch of specialisation that there is very little room left for the development of anything except individual technique. What between the sulphonamides, penicillin, and the antibiotics, almost every germ and virus, with one or two well-known exceptions, can be pin-pointed at once. In Surgery it is purely a matter of technique. But in mental work there is a whole new field of research open before us, where discoveries can be made every day. We are concerned with people's minds and personalities, even with their souls, and that is where the interest and thrill of mental work lies."

I had never been around the wards of a mental hospital and was very keen to do so. One Sunday morning the Deputy Matron, not the one I have just quoted, took me with her on her rounds. One of the drawbacks of my job is the fact that we are on duty from nine to five, and so have very little opportunity of seeing anything of the other departments. I knew well enough what the wards in general hospitals look like, but the wards of a mental hospital would be something quite new.

Miss Hickson was a charming, kindly little person, and appeared to know and love each patient individually. She could only take me round the Female Side, of course. The Male Side was under the jurisdiction of the Chief Male Nurse.

Each ward consisted of the whole of the ground floor or first floor of a huge wing, all radiating from the central block. Each was divided into three enormous rooms, one a dormitory, one is a dining room, and one a day room, or lounge, and each ward was a separate community on its own. Quite recently the old Poor Law system of numbering the wards had been abandoned, and each one had its own name. This system is now almost, though not quite, universal in mental hospitals, and the fact of having names rather than numbers has been proved to have a most remarkable psychological effect on both patients and staff. To be on "Nightingale" or "Lister" has a far more human and home-like sound than to be on "Male 3" or "Female 5". In one hospital I know, where the patients nearly all come from local areas, the wards are named after those districts, and it pleases the patients immensely if they happen to be in a ward of the same name as their home area. In another hospital, where most of the patients come from London, the wards are named after well-known and famous persons who are connected with London. When the naming system was introduced in their particular hospital, the Medical Superintendent himself wrote a short article on each of the characters in turn, in the hospital magazine. Where there is no special feature, either in personalities or districts, for which names can be given, it is very usual to name them after famous people connect with the medical world. No matter who, or what, the wards are named after, the mere fact of having names immediately introduces a warm and friendly atmosphere and encourages the patients to develop a sense of "belonging" which is quite impossible in the frigid atmosphere of numbers.

Once everyone has become accustomed to new names, all is plain sailing. But on one occasion I was working in a hospital during the period of transition from numbers to names. All the patients' cards and containers, as well as all the ward baskets and stock bottles, were still marked with the numbers. All the staff were still mentioning their wards by the numbers, but the edict had gone forth that names were to be used starting from now, and the ensuing confusion was quite incredible, particularly to the unfortunate locum - me.

Miss Hickson introduced me to each of the Sisters as we entered her ward, and everywhere I was given a genuinely warm welcome, and made to feel how pleased they were to have someone new to show round, and to admire their ward and charges. The dormitories were empty of patients, clean, light and airy, with bright coloured covers on the beds, pretty curtains, and flowers everywhere. The dining rooms were attractively set out with small tables for four or six, covered with white or coloured cloths. There were pictures everywhere on the walls, mostly of children, animals, or flowers studies. The living rooms were extremely attractive. There were numbers of big easy chairs, settees, cosy fireside chairs, book shelves and occasional tables. Many of them possessed a piano, and every one of them had gaily embroidered chair-backs and wool rugs, made by the patients themselves. The atmosphere everywhere was light with colour and sunshine, and the sense of kindliness and loving care. There was nothing whatever of the dreariness and drabness which I had anticipated. Nurses and cadets were moving among the patients, helping them with a bit of knitting, writing a letter for one or another, or carefully feeding some helpless soul with her mid-morning glass of milk. It was an absolute eye-opener to me.

Presently we came to the Geriatric ward. Most people know by now that Geriatrics are those feeble old people who used to be known as "Old Seniles." In this ward every bed was occupied by a still quiet old figure. All the bed covers were white, and the impression was almost like going into a Church. The Sister, a stout motherly type in her fifties, bustled forward to meet us.

"You must come and meet Grannie," she said. "She is the oldest patient in the hospital; she is ninety-eight and from the Registers we know that she has been here for over seventy years. She is a good one," she went on, emphatically, "she is never a bit of trouble, she takes her food like a lady, and" - the final accolade - "I have never known her with a soiled bed, and I have been on this ward over thirty years."

She led me to a corner of the ward, which was decorated almost like a shrine. Flowering plants in wall baskets hung around the corner, more flowers stood on the bedside locker, and a charming figure of the Madonna and Child hung above the head of the bed. In the bed lay the tiniest and frailest old lady I had ever imagined. The blue-veined eye lids were closed, and the thin, transparent hands were folded on the sheet. It might have been the figure of a saint carved in translucent alabaster. I hardly dared breath in the presence of such age and fragility.

"Isn't she lovely", I whispered, "I must not disturb her if she is asleep." "She is not asleep," said the Sister, "she spends most of her life lying quiet like this, but I always know when she is asleep, as her breathing changes." "What is her name"? I asked. "Maudie," was the answer, "but everyone calls her Grannie, though she has never been married, of course. Hold her hand and speak to her; she won't understand, but she loves to have her hand held and to hear someone's voice."

I was overcome by a wave of totally unaccustomed nervousness, but Sister put her great broad hand gently on Grannie's two tiny ones, and said, "Open eyes, Maudie, here's a lady come to see you." I leaned over the bed and took one skeleton hand in mine. I was half afraid my gentlest touch might crush it. Fumbling for my words, I said, "Hullo, Maudie. Sister has brought me to say how-do-you-do to you. She says you are good, and the best patient she has ever had." There was a tiny indrawn breath, then the delicate eyelids lifted and a pair of faded, vacant blue eyes looked up at me. As I watched I could see the faint glow of intelligence dawning in them. Sister at my shoulder, gave a gasp of delight. "She is taking notice of you", she exclaimed in a whisper, "it is very seldom she does that." Then the free hand began to waver upwards, like a fluttering white moth. Sister was thrilled. "She can see the sun on your hair," she said, "bend down lower, she wants to touch it".

Sister seemed to have the thought-reading capacity of a mother towards her baby. I am very pale, flaxen blonde, and the sun was streaming in across the bed. I bent down closer and the little hand moved feebly in my hair. "It’s like silk", came an almost inaudible whisper, "an' 'tis all gold. Be you an angel come to take poor old Maudie home at last?"

I do not cry easily, but I felt the tears flooding my eyes.

"No, sweetheart," I managed to reply, my cheek against her forehead, "I am not an angel. But very soon a real angel will come for you, and he will be far, far more beautiful than I could ever be."

Already the brief flicker of intelligence was fading, and the eyelids dropped again. But on the sweet old face was a faint smile which had not been there before. I kissed her gently and turned away, wiping my eyes and feeling rather a fool. Sister's big hand slapped me on the shoulder, and I found her looking at me as if I were a thaumaturge. "No need to be ashamed of a few tears," she exclaimed in her hearty voice, "that was a real miracle you did, if ever I saw one. Never in all the years I have known Maudie has she ever taken that much notice of anyone or spoken so many words at one time. She won't be able to say anything, but I warrant she'll never forget you".

By the time for my next visit to that hospital came around, the Angel had called for dear old Maudie, and her long, clouded life on earth had given place to that radiant life which she had waited so long and so eagerly.

CHAPTER 4

It might be thought that the work in hospital pharmacies would follow the same pattern throughout, and there would be very little variety. I thought so myself till I started my life as a locum. So far, I have worked in more than twenty-five different hospitals, and each one has an entirely different atmosphere and personality. About the only constant factors are the actual drugs themselves. In the Devon hospital I see quite a lot of the patients, and am on friendly terms with the whole staff, from Matron downwards, but I found things totally different in another hospital where I spent four weeks one summer.

The hospital consists of an old building, which used to be the original hospital, but during the war it was enormously enlarged by the addition of vast sprawling corridors with huge single floor blocks, Army style. It is completely characterless, but in spite of that I had an extremely amusing time there. The Matron was one of the aloof type, and the staff were inclined to follow her lead. The pharmacy staff was a close-knit compact little entity, on very good terms among themselves, and all united against the assaults and onslaughts of the rest of the staff. The Chief pharmacist was a real father to his staff, and one of the best champions of pharmacy that I have ever met. He expected his staff to show every civility and courtesy to members of other departments but defended them like a raging lion if any other department trod on any of our toes. I only saw him for the first morning as I was doing locum for him, and he put off his departure in order to show me round. He was not English, though he had the full English qualifications. He had spent a great part of his working life in his own country, on the Continent, where pharmacists and pharmacy have a far higher status than in England; but he saw to it that his department got far more respect than I have met with in a great many hospitals.

Many hospital pharmacies are small, cramped and old-fashioned. A very great deal of enlargement and reconstruction is going on everywhere, but it seems that invariably the pharmacy is the last department to get any attention or improvement. In this hospital, however, the pharmacy was the largest, finest and best equipped that I have seen anywhere, and that goes for all the London hospitals, some with world-famous names, in which I have worked. The old Chief had acquired this by sheer personality, and fearless bullying of the Management Committee. Most English pharmacists are far too retiring and long-suffering. They are still under the influence of the old days, when pharmacy was a vocation, before the Health Service came in. The other departments, Physiotherapy, Radiography and the rest, are new-fangled upstarts by comparison with the pharmacy. Yet, because they will get up and shout, they always get new apparatus and equipment and buildings and all they want; whereas the pharmacy, which is actually the nerve-centre of the whole hospital, can go hang. The pharmacy has always been there, ever since any hospital was first built and long, long before any of these other departments was ever dreamed of. The pharmacist of today traces his/her professional ancestry back through the old Apothecaries, alchemists, Monastic Infirmarians, and, hand in hand with the Physicians, back to Avicenna, Galen and the great Hippocrates himself. Before Hippocrates we can count the real person of Aesculapius, who after his death was worshipped as the Greek god of Medicine, and right back to Im-Hotep the Egyptian, and before him to Sekhet and the ancient drug-masters of Sumerian times.

In spite of the Health Service and the Welfare State, and the attendant, though inevitable soullessness which has come in their wake, we pharmacists still have a remembrance of the ancient ideals of unselfish service, and the sense of honour which we absorbed unconsciously with the touch of our first pestle and mortar. We are only Civil Servants now, but the spirit of our predecessors still hovers over us and makes us slow to get up and shout for our rights, or to claim the improved conditions which are given so free-handedly to others. I have myself worked, and seen scores of my colleagues working, under conditions which no Trades Unionist would countenance for a moment.

The pharmacy in this hospital however, was the complete answer to the pharmacist's prayer. It occupied almost the whole of one of the big blocks. There were large windows down both sides, wide, spacious working benches, six or eight sinks at convenient intervals with hot and cold water, and a properly constructed and enclosed sterilising room, which could be kept sterile - unlike so many so-called sterilising rooms I have known, where the plaster is peeling off the walls, the paint-work grimed with years of steam, and the ancient autoclave threatening to explode at any moment.

The main drug store and stock room was in the same block, and not down stairs in a cobwebby basement, miles away, as is the usual case. All the apparatus was clean and up to the minute, and above all there was plenty of space on the shelves for all the bottles. Ordinarily the shelves are so overcrowded that the bottles have to be packed in, several rows deep, and standing one on top of the other. The amount of time wasted and extra work involved in first, locating, then extricating, any required bottle is quite incredible, not to mention the irritation, frustration and nerve strain when one is already overwhelmed with work.

It was largely due to the excellent lay-out of this pharmacy that I found the work at this hospital easier than I have known anywhere. Everything was so beautifully arranged and so excellently tabulated that I could find practically anything I wanted by the end of the first day. It is not the fault of the pharmacist that almost every pharmacy is grossly over-crowded, and consequently impossible to keep tidy, except in so far as he is too self-effacing and long-suffering to stand up to the Management Committee and demand his rights. I am always reading the Riot Act to my colleagues and preaching to them the fact that times have changed. We are no longer three a penny, we are in urgent demand and, that being the case, we are in a stronger position than has been known in the profession for a very long time, perhaps ever.

My two assistants were the most unusual and fascinating that I have ever had. One was a Hungarian girl, and the other an Austrian man, both about twenty-five or so. Each was a qualified pharmacist in their own country. The girl and her husband had escaped and come to England in the autumn uprising in 1956. He was a doctor and had got a post in another hospital not far away, and they were hoping to get a flat and start their home together shortly. Meantime she was living in the hospital. She was in the throes of studying for the modified examination of the Pharmaceutical Society, which all pharmacists who have their own countries' qualifications, are required to pass before they can be recognised in England. The Austrian man was only over for a few months and was not trying for the English qualification. He was merely here for experience. He was not there when I arrived but turned up a few days later.

When the Chief took me into the pharmacy the first morning, the Hungarian girl was sitting at the bench immersed in the usual old job of counting tablets. She stood up as we came in, and I thought she was never going to stop standing up. She was quite the tallest woman I have ever seen. She towered a good head and shoulders above me, but she had such a perfect figure, long-legged and in beautiful proportion, that her height merely drew attention to her beauty. She had a mane of thick dark russet-brown hair, which was sketchily tied back, Alice-fashion, by a strip of frayed bandage; her lipstick and matching nail varnish were a deep mauve, which would have looked atrocious on an English girl, but which were in perfect keeping with her strange, exotic type. She had the broad cheek-bones and long eyes of the Magyar, and the wild untameable spirit of her people glowed unmistakably behind her perfect manners and preliminary shyness.

When she was introduced to me she gave a charming half curtsey, accompanied by a nervous smile and appealing glance from her strange eyes, and somehow gave the impression - which she often did afterwards - that despite her great advantage in height she was actually looking up at me. As soon as the shyness wore off, which it did very soon, I found her simply vibrating with personality, and utterly loveable. One moment she would be coaxing round me like a kitten, the next moment stamping round the pharmacy incoherent with fury over some small mishap or irritation, and when I laughed at her tantrums, the tears would immediately stream down her cheeks, and she would either fling herself face downwards across the bench, or else on my shoulder, wailing that her darling Meesis Ropair was unkind to her and didn't love her.

Her own Hungarian surname was quite beyond the capacity of English tongues, and she was invariably known as Tiny, for obvious reasons. On her arrival in England neither she nor her husband had a word of English, and for some weeks her only means of communication with the Chief was by means of pharmaceutical Latin. His native tongue was German, he knew a bit of French, and had an amazing command of English. But Hungarian had no basic affinity with any other European language as far as I can make out. With a knowledge of English and Latin one can usually get some sort of a grasp of most of the European languages, as they are almost all based on either Latin or Teutonic, but with Hungarian there is nothing whatever that one can get hold of. Tiny had only been in England about eight or nine months when we first met, but her knowledge of English was quite remarkable, both in scope and quality. Grammar, pronunciation, moods, tenses, or any semblance of correct phraseology, nothing whatever mattered to Tiny as long as she got her meaning across. She would hammer away for any length of time, getting more and more excited and eventually furious with frustration, but she always made herself understood in the end.

It was the same if words or idioms were used which she could not understand. She would worry away at them, sometimes for days, but she always got the meaning eventually. Her pronunciation was a sheer joy, and she had not the slightest inhibition about using the most outlandish words which she happened to have heard or read. She would take a flying shot at them and leave her hearers to pick up the pieces. "Th" was either "t", "d", "s" or "z", used quite indifferently, while "ing" was invariably "ink" or "inks". She adored the joke against herself when her remarks, quite unintentionally, reduced us all to hysterics. She was the complete extrovert, sizzling with brains, character and personality, and possessed of the most persistently inquiring mind. She was the "Elephant's Child" par excellence, consumed with 'satiable curiosity about every aspect of life. There was never a dull moment when Tiny was around.

She soon came to look upon me as a mixture of dictionary, encyclopaedia, Mother Confessor, and pharmacist's vade mecum, and it took me every minute of my time to keep up with her.

Ernst, the Austrian lad, was Tiny's complete antithesis. He was even taller than she was, and they both attached themselves to me like limpets. I adored them both, and alternately bossed and petted the two giants as if they were my kid sister and brother. Ernst had an extremely good knowledge of English, learnt at school. His pronunciation and grammar were almost faultless, but the poor boy was so intensely shy and nervous that he literally hardly dared open his mouth. He was as keen as Tiny to learn new English words and phrases, but every time he tried to say anything one could see his mind going blank with sheer nervousness, and the perspiration would start all over his face. He invariably appeared from nowhere as soon as Tiny and I began one of our involved question and answer sessions, with his note-book, pencil and pocket dictionary and phrase book at the ready. While Tiny was plunging head first into the English language, like a bull at a gate, there was always a faint murmur going on the in background, where Ernst was inaudibly correcting her. If Tiny ever happened to hear him doing so, she would explode in incoherent fury, while I laughed helplessly at both of them. Ernst did not do this with any idea of making any impression on Tiny, it was purely for his own edification.

Besides my two baby giraffes there was also a sweet little Irish girl, unqualified but extremely competent, and an elderly porter, an ex R.S.M. At midday dinner we were always joined by the hospital Secretary and his Assistant, two charming men, and we made up a most cheerful and noisy gang. They spent the rest of the dinner hour with us, either in the grounds, or in a cosy huddle in the pharmacy.

There was a fairly prolonged heat wave during the time I was there, and Tiny spent most of her spare time sun-bathing. She adored the sun, and equally abominated the rain. Most Hungarians seem to have this hatred of rain, and Tiny's pantomime and accompanying commentary of an English queue standing in the pouring rain waiting for a bus, was one of the funniest things I have ever witnessed. Another thing she could not get used to was what she considered our politeness. She had noticed that if any old person whose place was at the head of the queue, had left it and gone to rest on a nearby seat, all the remainder of the queue would wait when the bus arrived and allow the old person to get on first. She couldn't understand this attitude. Apparently, in Hungary it was a case of "you shove - I shove - we all shove" when it came to getting on a bus.

The work went on so smoothly and easily that the bulk of it was finished by one o'clock. During the afternoon Tiny had permission to sit down and study, while the rest of us dealt with all the extra oddments that came in. She was ploughing her way through a truly fearsome text-book on Forensic Medicine. It is an appalling work, phrased in the most complex legal language, often so involved that even I frequently had to read some sentence or paragraph several times before I could grasp what it was intended to mean. Tiny's courage and persistence in attacking this intimidating volume, made me marvel. She worked through it page by page, with the aid of her dictionary, translating it word for word into Hungarian, in double columns in her note book, to the accompaniment of moans, wailings and frequent tears; but she never gave up. My troubles started when she began to realise that I was ready to help her.

There was a big bench down the centre of the pharmacy, as well as others all-round the walls. The centre bench was divided down the middle by open racks of bottles. During the afternoons Tiny spread herself and her books down one side, while I spent a good deal of the time sitting at the other side dealing with invoices, entries and orders and all the vast amount of paperwork which falls to the lot of the Chief.

At frequent intervals I was interrupted by a soft appealing voice. "Meesis Ropair, may I ask you somesinks?" and looking up would see Tiny's anxious face peering at me between the intervening bottles. Then would ensue a brain-twisting session, as I tried to explain in Basic English the involutions and convolutions of Legal English. Quite often I found that Tiny had been able to translate into Hungarian every single word of the sentence in question, but the phraseology had her completely foxed. She was not the only one either. However it polished up my knowledge of Forensic Pharmacy in the most remarkable way. And always, in the background, was Ernst, following everything intently, making copious notes, and murmuring inaudible corrections to Tiny's spate of words. But Tiny never gave up. Tears flowed, and my brain felt as if it were being passed through a spin-drier, but she would never relax, or allow me any peace, till she had got the full meaning. Then her brilliant smile broke through the tears, there was a squeal of delight, and a bit of peace for me till the next problem arose.

Quite our worst and most complicated session was in connection with a dead mouse, and I confess I brought it on myself. It was Monday morning after a scorching weekend, and still grilling hot. An agitated little nurse dashed in panting.

"We've got a dead mouse and can you do something about it?" I am fully broken in to the most impossible demands, but this was a new one on me.

"I wouldn't know anything about a dead mouse," I replied cagily, "we don't handle dead mice here in the pharmacy."

"Oh, please, you must," she cried desperately, "it's down behind the hot pipes and the brush cupboard on the ward and we can't get at it even with a broom handle and someone left the pipes turned on all the weekend and you know how hot it's been and the ward maid nearly fainted when she went to the cupboard and then she vomited all over the floor and Sister's furious and Oh, you must do something or all the patients will start vomiting too."

I did a bit of brisk thinking. The situation on the ward was obviously getting out of hand. But all the same I wasn't going to get mixed up with a very dead mouse, not if I knew anything about it.

"You had better go along to the Maintenance Office," I said, "they can cope with dead mice better than the pharmacy can." Meantime, unknown to me, Tiny had crept up and was listening intently.

"Mices!" she exclaimed, dead mices" One meenit, Meesis Ropair, I get somesinks." And off she dashed. The next moment she was back with a tin of disinfectant powder. I took it and had a quick look at the label.

"Good girl," I said. "Here you are," I said to the nurse, "that will help to kill the smell but go to the Maintenance Office and get them to send a man to remove it."

The nurse grabbed the tin and fled, and as the door banged behind her, I remarked to the empty air, "That mouse must be singing it's swan song to high heaven by now".

I was aware of Tiny's long, brilliant eyes fixed searchingly on me, while invisible question marks danced round her head like a halo. But it was Monday morning, and we were very busy.

"Come on, Tiny," I exclaimed, "work's waiting. Run!" And we ran. In the rush of work I clean forgot the whole incident. Not so Tiny, not by any manner of means.

(Note:- within twenty-four hours of writing the above I received a letter from "Tiny" telling me that she had just passed her exam, and now holds the English qualification.)

That afternoon she and I were sitting, one on either side of the big bench, she immersed in Forensic Medicine, I in a pile of invoices. All was peace for a time. Presently I began to be aware that a certain amount of sighing and fidgeting was taking place on the other side of the rack of bottles. I took no notice, knowing perfectly well that very soon would come the plaintive appeal. Sure enough, it came.

"Meesis Ropair, may I ask you somesinks?

I hardened my heart and went on checking invoices.

Again, more softly and pleadingly came the appeal.

"Not now, I'm busy," I said sternly. "Did that delivery come in from Savory and Moore this morning?"

"Yes," all eagerness to please.

"Did you check the goods and put them away?"

"Yes."

"Well, where is the delivery note?"

"I put 'im on ze file," oozing conscious virtue.

"Oh, you remembered for once, did you? You usually get them mixed up with the invoices, and I was wondering why I hadn't come across it."

I finished my job, slapped the invoice file shut, and turned my attention to the anxiously watching face behind the bottles.

"Now then, what's your little worry this time?"

"Ees not leetle vorry," she replied sombrely, "ees vair' beeg worry. Meesis Ropair, tell me please, ees Eenglish mices all the same like Hungarian mices?"

The inevitable Ernst had materialised from nowhere, all ears and note-book.

I pondered the question solemnly. "I couldn't say for certain," I replied, "I have never made a study of mice of any sort. But I should think it more than likely that English and Hungarian mice are fairly similar."

Tiny drew a deep breath. Hurdle No. 1 was passed, and I waited for the next.

"Tell me," she said, still more earnestly, "does mices sink?"

"Well, " I replied carefully, "it depends upon what you mean by 'sink'. Do you mean 'think' - what you are supposed to do with your head, or do you mean 'sink' - what you do in the sea if you can't swim, or do you mean 'sing' - la-la-la?

"The question is now - do mice sing?" I said, trying hard to keep some semblance of coherence in the conversation. Ernst meanwhile taking rapid notes between murmured corrections. "To the best of my knowledge I should say, No. I believe there is a particular breed of mice in China or Japan known as singing mice, which are kept as pets, but we'll skip that. There are also the waltzing mice used by Mendel in the establishment of his theory of heredity, but we'll skip those too."

Ernst nodded vigorously, and muttered "establishment of the Mendelian theory", in perfect English. I waited for the next onslaught.

"Meesis Ropair, I ask you, what is SCHVONSONK?"

The question came like a javelin. I clasped my head between my two hands and rocked it tenderly too and fro.

"Tiny dear", I replied, "my middle name is George Washington, I cannot tell a lie. I haven't a clue."

"What is George Vashinktonk?" she demanded wrathfully "I not ask nozzinks about George Vashinktonk. I ask what is schvonsonk."

"George Washington, first President of the United States: noted for his truthfulness," in rapid sotto voice from Ernst.

"Be quiet, you Ernst," screamed Tiny, in fury, "go away; you bozzer me."

"Steady now," I said, seeing the tears rising. "Take it easy Tiny and try to explain just what you are trying to say."

"Zis mornink," she said, slowly and carefully, "zat dead mice", ("mouse" from Ernst). "You say mice sink schvonsonk. Now you say mices not sink, and you not know what is schvonsonk." She gazed at me with deep reproach. "I am only one poor schtewpid Hungarian Refugee girl, and I ask my so kind Meesis Ropair who schpeak so clear, so educate' ze Eenglish, and she no, not will tell me what is schvonsonk."

The incident of the dead mouse, and my thoughtless remark, flashed back to my mind. I laid my head on the invoices, choking with laughter.

"Now you laugh at me," came the reproachful voice, "I ask a question you say you not know nozzinks, and now you laugh. You not loff me no more - I go avay, schvollow two-three tablets, and fft! - no more Tiny."

"Don't be a little mutt," I said, pulling myself together. "Listen carefully, now, and I will explain. Ernst, scenting the disclosure of still more mysteries of the English language, edged closer, breathing hard down the back of my neck.

"You know what is a swan?" I asked. "A big white bird," I flapped my arms in illustration. "it swims on the water and has a long neck, like that." I held my hand and forearm in imitation of a swan's neck and head. Tiny recognised my meaning at once. Her face lit up, and she exclaimed the word for swan in her own language. I went on - "There is an old legend, a story, that swans never sing or make any sound until the moment they are dying," (scribble, scribble went Ernst's pencil) "so in English we call the very last action anyone makes before they die, their swan song."

"Aiee" came in a squeal of delight from Tiny, as comprehension dawned. But immediately she sobered again.

"You say zat mouse go to Heaven," she said gravely. "I know what is Heaven. Izz Good Place. Up zere", she pointed to the ceiling. "Is zat vair' good mouse, he go to Heaven?"

"No dear," I said nearly at the end of my tether, "I didn't say the mouse was going to Heaven. I meant the dreadful smell was the mouse's swan song, and it was so strong that it would go right up to the sky. Now, do you see what I meant?

Tiny grasped it at last. Her face alight and a dozen Magyar devils dancing in her brilliant eyes, she exclaimed all in one breath, "Mice dead! Mice smells bad go right up to Heaven make angels schneeze!" Then on a triumphant top note - "Mice SCHTINKS"!

CHAPTER 5

Living conditions and food vary as much from one hospital to another as the pharmacies and colleagues do. In the Devonshire hospital, the food is superb and my quarters luxurious, but the pharmacy is small, cramped and out of date, and apart from my golden-hearted Will, and occasional very youthful cadets, I am single-handed.

In the hospital, where I had Tiny and Ernst and numerous other experienced helpers, and a show-place of a pharmacy, the food was atrocious and the living accommodation adequate, but only just.

Seen from the air, the new part of the hospital must look like a centipede. The head is near the old building, while the long main corridor sprawls endlessly all over the grounds, with the big single-storey blocks sticking out like legs all the way down each side. A number of the blocks at the far tail and were given over to staff bedrooms. Each of these blocks had a central corridor opening off the main corridor, with scores of little cell-like rooms on each side. The wash rooms were all at one end. I was there in the summer when the blocks were like furnaces, but in winter they must be like refrigerators. The wash basins were all open together, no washing privacy except if one could snaffle one of the three bathrooms, and even in summer on chilly days, howling draughts swept up and down the corridor. It was just like being in the Army again. Another block near the bedroom blocks, was the Staff Recreation Room. This was a huge, gaunt place with small bleak tables and chairs in one part, and at the far end a few arm chairs and settees grouped round the T.V. Very few of the staff used the Rec: Room, as most of them shook the dust of the place off their feet at the moment they came off duty. We met them in giggling shoals making tracks for the nearest dance hall or cinema.

I was not given my status as ranking with the Sisters, though this did not worry me in the least. The Sisters were a snooty lot, and I was far happier spending my off duty with Tiny and Ernst and one or two of the Male Charge Nurses. We made up our own little gang, and if I happened to stop in my room after supper writing letters before joining them at the T.V., I invariably found the best chair had been secured and put in the centre of the circle for me. To make quite sure that no one else would take it, I usually found that either Tiny or Ernst was sitting in their own chair, with their long legs draped sideways over the one that was being kept for me.

If the Sisters were snooty, the Staff Nurses were completely mannerless. There was one in particular whom Tiny loathed. She was a fat, stocky little party, and unfortunately, she lived in and was technically in charge of, the block where my bedroom was. She never missed an opportunity of being rude to me whenever we met and would bawl at me down the length of the corridor, using my surname only, just as she did at the juniors. My reply to this was to be completely deaf until she gave me the "Mrs." when I would answer her with the most exquisite politeness, and if possible using the longest words I could think of, knowing perfectly well that she understood nothing more than the basest form of Basic English. She was English, I am sorry to say, as she was a remarkably unpleasant specimen of the breed, and a very large number of her juniors were either Colonial or Continental. Tiny, however, was quite cute enough to recognise her for what she was.

Tiny and I were chatting in my corridor one evening, near the swing doors. This Staff Nurse came barging along, pushed us both roughly aside as she banged through the swing doors, letting them fly back nearly hitting us. Tiny glared after her wrathfully and exploded,

"Zat is ze mostest oneducate' vimmins in ze hospitahl."

My only reaction was to say I couldn't agree more. She could not have expressed my sentiments more neatly.

Both Tiny and Ernst were Canasta fans, and both of them very good players. I had never had an opportunity of learning Canasta and had always been keen to do so. They joyously undertook to teach me. As every Canasta player knows it is not a very easy game to learn in all its ramifications, and my sufferings on being taught in a mixture of very incoherent Hungarian-English, interpolated by usually correct Austrian-English, which however came adrift badly in the excitement of the game, were quite incredible.

Ernst's shyness evaporated under the stimulus of Canasta, but with the shyness the careful correct English also disappeared. He and Tiny spluttered and exploded in a haze of incoherence. The fourth in the party was a very nice Charge Nurse, called Harold.

His knowledge of Canasta was only slightly better than mine, and Tiny and Ernst were in the seventh heaven with two novices to instruct. The scoring, quite tricky at the best of times, invariably became a perfect riot when conducted in an assortment of different languages. Tiny never attempted to calculate in English but reverted immediately to Hungarian. Ernst did likewise in German. Not to be outdone, I contributed voluble French and a horrible compound of German and Dutch, while Harold added the final bouquet to the pot-pourri by coming up with some Arabic, picked up during his war service.

I have never played Canasta in all-English company and am still wondering if my phraseology of the game is correct, or merely the literal translation from Hungarian and German.

People often ask me how I get my nonstop sequence of locum jobs. They seem to think there is a central agency for pharmacists like a kind of typists' pool. But there is nothing of the sort, though the formation of a locum pool has occasionally been discussed in the Society. The main snag is the acute scarcity of the locums, and the enormous demand for them. I have always found my own jobs through the columns of the Pharmaceutical Journal, and I pick them mainly on the principle of locality. I am almost invariably asked to go again, and I don't flatter myself that it is on account of my charm or efficiency; it is merely because, having once got hold of a locum, they are so desperate that they will hold on to them at any price. Short, that is, of complete imbecility or hopeless inefficiency. By

nnow I have built up a circuit which keeps me going most of the year, but I always like to try out one or two new hospitals each season, by way of variety.

By picking my jobs of the principle of locality I mean that if I happen to want to see some particular town or area I reply to an advertisement there, and hope for the best. In this way I have got about to a lot of places which I should never otherwise have seen. Granted, it is a complete toss-up as to where I land, and what sort of work and accommodation I let myself in for, but it is only for a few weeks in any case, and any discomfort or over work is worthwhile for the sake of seeing a new town or area. In self-defence I must say that this is not my only object in doing locum work, but it adds considerably to the interest.

It was on this principle that I took a post in a general hospital in a certain town. (Hemel Hempstead, Hertfordshire – JFH) The reason for my choice was that my Father had been in practice there as a young man just after qualifying. It was there also that my Mother had been Assistant Matron under her own eldest sister who was Matron of a hospital where my Father was visiting consultant. It was there that my parents first met, married, had their first home, and my sister and two elder brothers were born. They had moved to London where my Father set up in practice in the West End before I was born, but the name of this town was familiar to me from my earliest days. My Father's family and forebears had lived in and around this district for generations, and, being very ancestor conscious, I knew a great deal about them and their doings from my parents, though I had only once been taken to this town as a very small child and had no recollection of it whatever. The advertisement for a locum pharmacist in the hospital there was the realisation of a lifelong dream of visiting the district and indulging in a bit of ancestor hunting.

The hospital was in two buildings about a mile apart. The Nurses' Home in which I was to live was attached to the building on the far outskirts of the town, which had originally been the old Workhouse. Most of the old people had either been found other accommodation since the coming of the Health Service, or had died, and there was now only one block which housed about sixty of the original Workhouse inmates. These had no relatives to whom they could go, and most of them had spent so many years in the place that it would have been cruel to uproot them. They spent their time sitting in the gardens or living rooms, peacefully passing their last years under the care of an extremely pleasant and kindly Sister, with whom I became very good friends. All the other blocks or of the original Workhouse had been beautifully modernised and turned into wards, most of them being the district Maternity unit.

The Nurses' Home was superb. It had only been completed and opened about a year before I went there, and it was widely recognised as a model of what Nurses' living accommodation should be. It was built right out in the fields at the back of the hospital with open country all round. The rooms were beautifully decorated and furnished in contemporary style, with fitted basins, electric fires, bedside lights and every comfort. There was a wash room and hot cupboard where we could do our personal laundry, also an ironing room, and small kitchens where we could make ourselves cups of tea or get ourselves snack meals if we did not want to go over to the main dining room. These may seem unimportant items, but they add up to a very great deal where women are concerned. If more hospitals provided good and up to date amenities and comforts for their staff it would go far towards helping solve the problems of getting, and keeping, their Nurses. This hospital, the Devon hospital, and one other, are the only three examples of really good living conditions which I have met in all my experience. All the others range from moderately bearable, to downright disgraceful.

But however good the actual Nurses' Home maybe it is the Home Sister or Warden who makes or mars the entire place. Home Sisters are now being replaced to a great extent by Wardens which is all to the good. It is being realised that a trained Nurse is being wasted on the running of a Nurses' Home, as has so long been the case when Home Sisters are employed, . Wwhereas Wardens are not trained nurses but have usually had wide experience and training in Social Service and Domestic Science, and are therefore excellently fitted for such posts. All Wardens that I have met have been charming and most competent women, and in every case on their introduction to the charge of a Nurses' Home, improvements and better amenities have been brought in on their recommendations.

At this particular hospital there was still a Home Sister, and she was the maddest, craziest, most hot tempered, yet incredibly efficient little Irishwoman that could be imagined. She ran that place magnificently, bullied, bossed, petted and scolded the lot of us, wore herself out with tearing energy, and was either immensely popular, or whole-heartedly loathed. Personally, I got on marvellously with her, and came to love her dearly. She would chew my head off with as little compunction as she would the youngest junior, but she had a heart of solid gold, as long as one could find it under the extremely prickly exterior. At first, I did not quite know how to handle her, but soon learned that to take her scolding with a laugh and joke was the surest way to reveal that golden heart. Quite soon after my arrival, while I was still at the stage of approaching her with great weariness, I scalded my hand rather badly while working with the horrible old autoclave. It was my right hand and my efforts at bandaging it while at work were definitely unprofessional. When I got back in the evening I went along to Sister's office to ask her to do it for me. By the reception I got, one might have thought I had done it on purpose to annoy her. She was a tiny, thin little creature, with the explosive content of an H-bomb. She fairly flew at me, pouring forth streams of vituperation in a rich Irish brogue, while she bandaged my hand at supersonic speed, making a perfect demonstration job of it. I said not a word to her scolding but grinned at her as she strapped me up. When she had finished, I put my arm round her waist and whispered, "Thank you, love," in her ear. She glared at me for a moment, then an enchanting smile broke out and she patted me out of the office like a mother. Ever after that, we were the firmest of friends, and she would often pour out her woes and her tantrums to me, enormously to my amusement.

I found I was to share myself between this part of the hospital and the other, which was right down in the middle of the town. The Chief was on holiday during my first visit, and I was the only qualified. The pharmacy at St. Paul's, the old workhouse building, was quite small but very bright and new, with large, wide windows looking onto the grounds. As the building was almost entirely given over to Maternity and Ante-Natal work the dispensing could usually be finished by lunch-time. I worked there in the mornings with Miss Marsham, a cheerful and friendly girl, who was very experienced, though unqualified. After lunch I had to make my way down to the main hospital, where I spent the afternoons. It was not a comfortable arrangement as, unless I could catch the hospital van and get a lift, it meant a long walk there and a long walk back in the evening. Pharmacy is not the sort of job at which one can sit, or only very rarely, and the strain on one's feet is such that one avoids any extra walking like the plague. Unfortunately, the van driver was not a very co-operative or accommodating person. He knew perfectly well that I had to go down after lunch every day but as often as not he would make his call and clear off again without giving me a chance to catch him. Miss Marsham had her own car and went home to lunch. If there was anything left over to do at the end of the morning she went back to St. Paul's and finished off, then came down to the main hospital for the remainder of the day.

The first time I walked into the town on my way to the hospital, I was fascinated beyond words to recognise the names of roads of which I had heard my parents speak, and to see signposts with the names of outlying villages which I had known all my life. The town itself is one of those which is being almost completely rebuilt and modernised. The old main street was in the process of almost entire demolition for widening purposes, and apart from a few of the smaller and older side roads, and a hitherto untouched area by the Church, my parents would have been hard put to it to recognise their old home town. However, as I approached the main hospital, I suddenly saw a building which I felt convinced I knew. I stopped dead and stared. Yes, it was unmistakable. It was the old original hospital which I had seen in the photograph albums in my childhood. The hospital where my Aunt had been Matron, my Mother Assistant Matron, my Father visiting consultant, and where he had proposed to my Mother in the dispensary all among the bottles more than sixty years before. The old building was not incorporated in the new hospital and used, I believe, for offices and stores, but I found on subsequent enquiry, that it was indeed the old original hospital.

The main hospital was in the throes of being enlarged and modernised, but when I was there, the pharmacy was, as usual, being left till last. During the past year I have heard that the new pharmacy is almost completed, but when I was there, we were still working in the old pharmacy, under the most appalling conditions. It was in a semi-basement, the only outlook being directly on to high walls which only allowed the merest glimpse of sky, by dint of much craning of necks. It was so dark that on the sunniest days we always had to work by artificial light. It was far too small for the greatly increased bulk of work; the shelves were cramped and so over full that it was a perfect nightmare trying to find anything. When all the ward baskets were brought down there was not sufficient floor space for them to be brought into the pharmacy, and they had to be stacked in the corridor outside. This meant that we had to carry them in singly and take them out again when filled. There was no pharmacy porter, and ward baskets piled up with half a dozen Winchesters besides all the multitudinous ward stock bottles and individual patients' bottles, are far heavier than any woman should be expected to handle. I never attempted to lift them, but kicked and dragged them along the floor, and even so it took all my strength to move them.

The sterilising room was a disgrace. The paint and plaster were in such a shocking condition that any hope of attaining anything approaching sterile conditions was a sheer impossibility. All we could hope to do was to keep our coats and hands and apparatus as clean as possible and rely for sterility upon the autoclave. This was an old horror, dating from the dark ages. Miss Marsham and I often did the sterilising during the afternoons and we were both scared stiff of the old thing. She was far more used to it than I was, but she was even more scared than I. It would suddenly develop terrific pressures and blow off clouds of scalding steam from all the wrong apertures, the valves were so antiquated that it was a marvel that they did not explode, and the pressure gauges would leap and flicker up and down with not the slightest apparent connection with the actual temperature. However, it worked, if one had the nerve to handle it. The Chief had got it taped and would cope with its vagaries with the utmost aplomb, but it was the terror of my life, and I loathed having to have anything to do with it.

The stock rooms and dressings store were next door to the pharmacy, both of them so small and over-stuffed that it was a marvel that we ever found anything at all. In the stock room the bottles were stacked six or eight deep on the shelves and it doubled and trebled the work in finding things, besides requiring a high degree of acrobatics to reach them when found. Having no pharmacy porter, we ourselves, an all-woman staff, had to handle the huge five-gallon drums of methylated spirit, and the great containers of disinfectants, and do all the heavy work normally done by the porter.

The Chief, with whom I worked on a later visit, was an extremely nice girl in her thirties, a strong wiry type who spent her holidays skiing and rock climbing and in such like energetic and active pursuits. The assistant was another of the same physique, and neither of them thought anything of heaving the great ward baskets and drums of meths about. It was most unusual to find two women physically capable of doing this, and they both considered Miss Marsham and me as very weak and feeble specimens because we literally were completely unable to emulate them. Apart from that the Chief was very friendly and we soon made up a most cheerful and talkative party.

The assistant was a real character. She was a tiny little creature, a thin active little dynamo of energy. She was older than any of us, but had not a single grey hair, and could work any of us, even including the Chief, to a standstill. Having spent all the week on her feet, working at terrific speed, she spent her weekends with fellow members of a walking club, doing incredible mileages all over the neighbouring countryside. Her name was Miss Kitson, of course known as Kitsie, and to see Kitsie man-handling a drum of meth: or disinfectant almost as big as herself, was to witness a miracle of mind over matter. She had spent most of her life in the town and had worked at the hospital for an unbelievable number of years. She had never qualified, but she knew the work inside out and upside down. Chief pharmacists came and went, but Kitsie took them all in her stride, taught them the ropes, helped them through their teething troubles, and ran the whole show for them. She was a gay, chirpy, delightful little soul, and everybody knew and loved her. She had been there longer than any of the doctors, Sisters or senior staff, and had no hesitation in ticking them off, pulling their legs, giving them advice, and generally jollying them all round. She knew everybody in the town, likewise their sisters and their cousins and their aunts, unto the third and fourth generation. She was thrilled to pieces when I told her of my family's long-ago connection with the neighbourhood, and I found her a treasure house of information. Although my parents had left the town long before Kitsie's time, she dug round among her friends and, to my unutterable delight, actually found an elderly couple who had been patients of my Father's in their youth and gave me an introduction to them. I gave her the names of various others of my relations and she put me in touch with an old lady who proved to be a distant cousin several times removed. I called on the old lady, and we spent many happy evenings climbing up and down our family tree together.

Finding Kitsie such a marvellous local encyclopaedia I dug up from the depths of my memory the name of the house which had been my parents' first home. It was purely an echo of what I had been told in my childhood, but Kitsie pricked up her ears at once, and declared the name rang a bell. She went into a huddle with herself all among the bottles, working at high speed, but in quite unaccustomed silence for some time. Then she suddenly came to the surface.

"I've seen that name on a gatepost somewhere," she said, "I believe it is one of those big houses which are being demolished just down beyond here in the main road."

After work I went in accordance with her directions, and there, sure enough, was the name, cut deep into the capstone on the top of a pillar at the entrance to a drive. The demolition squads were at work, and the house was already in ruins, but enough of the front was still standing for me to be able to recognise it from the old photographs. It must have been a beautiful old Georgian house, and it is impossible for me to describe my feelings as I stood in the wrecked garden and looked at it. One of my curses is that I feel far more acutely about inanimate objects than I can about people. People have the gift of free will and can, to a great extent, make or mar their own lives, but so called inanimate objects are utterly helpless. They can be loved and cherished and thus given a personality and entity of their own; but with the departure or death of those that loves them they can be defaced, ruined, abandoned, or utterly abolished under the brutal callousness of the bull dozer or the commercial soullessness of the auctioneer's hammer. And they are utterly helpless. I sent out my heart to the poor old house and thereafter every day I went out of my way to go and visit it and send it my love and grief on its death agonies.

The next time I went to that hospital a few months later, there was nothing left but a huge raw gap. Everything had gone, and the capstone hearing the name was tumbled into the torn-up mud of what had been the drive. It was lying so that the name was still visible, and regardless of the passers-by I bent down and touched it gently in farewell. Sentimental? But that is how I am made. As my eldest brother, an extremely erudite clergyman once said to me in lofty tones, and true brotherly scorn, "Animism, my dear girl, sheer animism."

I In hospital one adopts a method of progression which can only be described as the hospital scuttle. No one actually runs, and for some reason running is frowned upon. It just isn't done. But everyone is so frantically busy and in such a desperate hurry to get from point A to point B in the shortest possible time, and we all scuttle about like a lot of clockwork mice. When I am at home, leading a civilised life, I walk in a fairly civilised manner, with reasonably high heels. But the moment I get into hospital and don on my white coat and flat heeled shoes, I immediately find myself scuttling with the best of them. It is an automatic reaction to the atmosphere of hustle and rush.

One day I was cruising down one of the corridors at the usual rate of knots, past a door with Board Room written in large and important letters upon it. I had passed that door scores of times, but hitherto it had always been closed. This time it was half open, and what I saw brought me up with a round turn. It stopped short in my tracks, all the breath taken out of me. There, on the wall, just seen through the half open door, was the portrait of my great uncle. It was a full-size print from an oil painting which I had known all my life.

I peeped round the door, and seeing the room was empty, I went in and stood for a long time gazing delightedly up into the handsome, benevolent, bearded face. I had never known him in the flesh, but the portrait was as familiar to me as my own hand. The eyes smiled into mine, and he seemed to say, "Well my dear, we meet again. I am in a place of honour among the Governors in the Board Room, and you are running about in a drug stained coat on your way to the basement. But your work is quite as important as any that I did here in the past, so keep heart, my child. We be of one blood, ye and I."

The walls of the room were lined with portraits of past Governors of the hospital, ranging back over more than a hundred years. All the others bore each a small plaque giving the name and years of office, but there was none on the portrait of my great uncle. On the advice of the Chief, I went to see the hospital Secretary, as the Chief told me there had always been a mystery about that portrait, and she knew he would be only too pleased to have any information I could give.

I found the Secretary intensely interested. He took notes of all that I could tell him and promised that an appropriate plaque should be placed on the frame. He then got out the early registers of the hospital and showed me. As we turned the pages, there, over and over again, in the lists of subscribers, Committee Members, Hospital Officers and Governors appeared the names of my ancestors in all the family ramifications for well over a century.

I scuttled back to the pharmacy in the dark, stuffy basement. I felt a glow of proprietary pride in the hospital which my forbears had helped to found so long ago, and which they had supported and directed for so many years.

Great Uncle Jack

John Evans KBC FRS
1823 – 1908

CHAPTER 6

One very great advantage in pharmacy work in mental hospitals is that it is only in very rare cases that one has Out Patients to cope with. I only know of one mental hospital where there are Out Patients, and that is the most highly specialised teaching hospital in the world of mental treatment. By the nature of things patients in mental hospitals have to be resident, though with the introduction of the new drugs and accompanying new methods of treatment, many of them are allowed to go home either permanently, or for specified periods.

On the other hand, in general hospitals, Out Patients form a very large and important part of our work. We all know perfectly well that this is the case, and in spite of what you - the Out Patients - may think to the contrary, it is a point of honour with us to give you the quickest possible service, and never to keep you waiting a moment longer than is necessary. But we find many of you a terrible trial. No Out Patient seems to have the slightest idea of the amount of work involved in putting up even the simplest box of tablets, let alone making up some special bottle of mixture or some unusual ointment. Over and over again I have had said to me, in varying tones of impatience and annoyance, "The doctor says it's only some tablets. Why can't I have them straight away?"

When one had a bench stacked up with previous O-P's prescriptions, all of which have to be worked through in strict rotation, remarks of this sort are trying to say the least of it.

As each prescription card is handed in, every new item has to be copied into the ledger, but before doing that it has to be deciphered. We seem to acquire some strange sixth sense when it comes to reading doctors' writing. We always get there in the end, but often many precious minutes are wasted before we can be sure that we are reading it correctly. And it is not only the actual drugs and directions which have to be deciphered; they, in fact, are often the easiest part, as the merest squiggle will usually put us on the track. The real snag is the patient's name. The names of the drugs are familiar to us, however badly written, but if the patient's name is nothing but a scrawl, we have no guiding light whatever. If one is working in an area where there are numbers of foreigners, our struggles are truly pitiable, although I will say that occasionally the name, in that case, is written in block capitals. Even so, it is frequently a toss-up as to which is the first name and which is the surname. If you get a name like Theodopulos Niarchos one might do as well as the other, for the surnames are sometimes written first, and sometimes second. Of course, one can always fall back upon asking the patient, but unless one spots an indecipherable name before the patient leaves the hatch, we are still further sunk, as it is impossible to call a patient whose name one cannot read. The O-P Sister does not welcome us with a friendly smile if we are obliged to go to her office and ask her. She is far too busy.

Having read the name and the prescription, and copied it into the ledger, a suitable container must be found, the label written, the tablets found and counted, or the mixture made up, the eye drops prepared and measured, the ointment weighed out, and the items labelled and finished off, ready to hand out. All this takes much longer than you - the Out Patient - can realise. It must also be remembered that some cards have several prescriptions all for the same person, which means that one patient takes as long to deal with as if each prescription had been for a different person. It is an age-old grouse among ourselves that O-Ps seem to think we can hand out their stuff like a barmaid pulling up drinks with a handle.

Another irritating habit which O-Ps have, is to adopt the attitude that we are bound to have made a mistake, or given them the wrong stuff, or put something poisonous into the mixture. The amount of suspicion and distrust to which we are subjected, is quite amazing. If a patient had been having a green mixture and some yellow tablets, the patient, as often as not, will announce in a loud and penetrating voice. "You have made a mistake. This is not the same as I had last time. You have given me the wrong stuff."

Thereby tending to alarm all the other waiting patients, and to undermine their confidence in us. We then have to waste more precious minutes in assuring the complainer that this is exactly what the doctor has ordered, that he has altered their prescription, and that they can be fully assured that no mistake has been made. And all the time more scripts are being handed in, and the work is piling up higher and higher.

We always do our utmost to show civility to the Out Patients, but we are only human, and it is little wonder if, under the strain of this sort of thing, repeated ad nauseam, we become slightly terse at times. After a certain amount of experience, we know exactly when to close an argument by firmly shutting down the hatch, or when it is advisable to tell the patient that if they are not satisfied they can take their card back to the doctor and see what he has to say about it. This will usually silence all but the most persistent grumbler, for they know they will get very short shrift from a busy and overworked doctor.

Of course, it is not by any means all O-Ps who make nuisances of themselves, but there is no getting away from the fact that there are far too many who do.

Another type of patient whom we find very annoying is the intelligent type, who wants to engage us in a long and confidential conversation as to the nature of the therapeutic action of the drugs on his/her prescription. This type will do their utmost to worm out of us exactly what the doctor has prescribed, why he has prescribed it, what it is composed of, and why it is to be taken before meals instead of after. To all these questions we invariably give blandly non-committal answers. It would be the grossest dereliction of our duty if we were to give any information whatever as to the doctor's diagnosis or prescribing. This of course gives the patient the impression that we are completely ignorant, and he goes off fuming indignantly about the low mentality and lack of education of those in the responsible position of making up his medicines for him.

The therapeutic action of drugs is not, strictly speaking, the concern of the pharmacist. Our job is to dispense the doctors' prescriptions; but it does not take us long before we know almost as much about the action of drugs as the doctors do. One glance at the patient's prescription card tells us exactly the nature of the complaint, as clearly as if it were all written out for us in large size capitals. Although we are not trained in diagnosis we can, after a bit of experience, and if we are sufficiently interested in that side of the job, come to recognise certain types of physique and appearance which indicate that the individual is either suffering from some particular complaint, or is a likely subject for it. Quite often if I am not too much rushed, I take a quick look at the patient before looking at their card and make an instantaneous mental diagnosis. By then looking at the card I can check as to whether I am correct or not. It is interesting to find how often I am right.

I must make it quite clear that the nature of the complaint is never written on the prescription cards. That appears only on the patient's case sheet or in the doctor's notes, which are no concern of ours, and which we never see unless for some very exceptional reason they have to be referred to. Our deductions are made simply and solely through our knowledge of the drugs we handle. Without giving away any professional confidences I think I may observe that diabetics are always of a very intelligent type, from whatever walk of life they come. They are invariably courteous and helpful, and quite one of the nicest types to deal with. Epileptics usually have a very gentle patient manner, and show a quite charming gratitude for our services. The neurotics are the worst, and one can often expect sparks to fly at a neurotic clinic.

At one such clinic there was a young woman who was well known as everybody's headache. In dispensing for these patients there was a rule, compared with which the Laws of the Medes and Persians were so much ephemerae. It was that, no matter for how many weeks the prescription was written up, we could not, under any circumstances, issue more than one week's supply. The patient only had to pay the one shilling on the prescription but had to come back each week to collect the stuff for as many weeks as it was ordered. The reason was that the type of drug was so potent, and the type of patient so unreliable that it was unsafe to issue the whole quantity at once. This particular patient had the pleasant habit of taking her whole week's supply in about three days, and then turning up again and demanding more. The doctors and nurses were in despair about her, and as for us in the pharmacy, she nearly drove us up the wall. One day she had come in after about three days clamouring for more tablets. The doctor came in and had a discussion with me before writing up her card. I put up the tablets he ordered and called the patient to the hatch to take them. She took one look at the glass phial of tablets and pushed them back to me, exclaiming, "Those are no good to me; I don't want those. I want the ones I had last time. You can take those and chuck them down the sink".

"I can't do that," I replied, "those are what the doctor has ordered for you this time, so you must go and talk to him if you are not satisfied."

She snatched up the phial and was just about to throw it at my head, when I slammed down the hatch just in time. Unknown to me, the Chief was just the other side of the hatch in the Out-Patient's Hall. A few moments later he came in with a grin all over his face, holding out something to me in his hand.

"Look here," he said, "just what I expected." It was the phial and tablets, smashed and stamped on.

"Good thing you shut the hatch down in time," he went on, "you would have got that right in your face. She flung it on the floor and jumped on it."

"She's a sweet soul, isn't she?" I said. "I hope I did the right thing insisting on her taking them."

"Quite right," he replied, "it will do her good. Now she will have to go to the end of the week without anything. The doctor won't give her any more after this exhibition."

Oh, yes, we definitely do see life through the hatch.

An ever-recurring question from every type of O-P is "How do I take it?" In tones varying from the querulous to the suspicious or indignant. If I had a shilling for every time I have said in what I hope is a civil and friendly voice, but which I fear is quite often bored or exasperated, "All the directions are on the label," I should be a rich woman by now.

The patient invariably stares at the label with still deeper suspicion, or else snorts indignantly and marches off, nose in the air.

This attitude of suspicion and distrust directed against pharmacists, is a very curious and noticeable feature of our relationship with the public. It is well known that the relationship of the doctor and patient has deteriorated sadly since the coming of the Health Service, but this attitude towards us pharmacists has nothing to do with the Health Service. It has existed since time immemorial. I am convinced that it is an ancient survival of the fear with which the alchemists and astrologers were regarded throughout the centuries. Our early predecessors were dabblers in the occult; by means of their drugs they could induce visions and dreams and steal a man's soul away from his body; and in their hands was the power of the unseen poison. The very word "Pharmacist" comes from a Greek word meaning "a poisoner, a sorcerer, a magician." Many other Greek words from the same root mean - to suffer from the effects of poison - to be ill or distraught - to administer a drug - to use enchantments - an enchanted potion - a charm - a spell - a stupefying drug - a sorceress - a witch. In the long list of derivations, all with the same evil portent, there are only one or two indicative of curative or remedial properties.

Right through the ages, to within living memory, the ingrained superstitious fear of the pharmacist, the poisoner, has held away in the minds of societies. I know. I have seen it over and over again, though no one would admit it, and would pour scorn on the very suggestion. But it is there. I have seen it in the eyes that peer into the pharmacy, that gaze in uncomprehending awe at our ranks of bottles with unimaginable names, at our delicate scales and tiny weights, at our glass measures and queer shaped flasks, and that watch in fascinated interest as our hands flick around among the drugs and apparatus. Our power of reading prescriptions is an unending source of wonder, and I have often seen that unconscious look of age old, semi superstitious awe flash for a moment in the eyes of my questioners.

Why is it that everyone loves to peer into the pharmacy? Nurses adore coming into the pharmacy, ward maids, porters, and above all the patients, if they get the slightest chance, will slide in and stand gazing about entranced, till we chase them out.

This attitude of fear is crystallised by the meaning generally attached to the word "drug". I use it throughout in its true sense, which is a medicament of any sort whatever. But to the general public the word immediately conjures up the horrors of what is known as "drug addiction" or "drug fiends". In its true sense the word covers numbers of substances running into thousands, but in the sense of addiction it is restricted to hardly more than a dozen at the very outside. All substances used for any form of medication, whether animal, vegetable, mineral or synthetic, are drugs. Even the simple indigestion tablets, or Syrup of Figs, come into the category.

All poisons and poisonous substances are covered by the most stringent legal regulations, but above all, those that can cause addiction are the most tightly controlled. And that is our responsibility.

The payment of a shilling on each prescription is another headache for us. The Out Patients are very good about paying up, apart from the preliminary grumbles when the payment was altered from a shilling per script to a shilling per item, but our trouble is concerned with the actual collecting of the shillings. Different hospitals have different methods of collection. In some hospitals we are provided with a float of change, and all the O-Ps have to do is to give us the money. We can give them any change required, and we stick the stamps on the sheets ourselves. The sheets are then collected by Finance each day, and the stamps checked off against our cash. This is by far the best method. In other hospitals there is a slot machine in the O-P department alongside the hatch, and into this the patients put their own money, and hand us the stamps or tickets. We have no change in the pharmacy and do not handle any money at all. This method is a ceaseless cause of annoyance both to ourselves and to the patients. They never, by any chance, have the required coins to put in the slot machine, and are everlastingly asking us for shillings. The amount of time wasted by us and the patients under this method, is quite incredible. A patient appears at the hatch, hands in the card, and feebly waves a ten-shilling note at us.

"I haven't got a shilling. Can you give me some change?" comes in a querulous bleat.

"I am so sorry, we don't supply change here. You may be able to get some at the canteen," we reply firmly, and for about the fiftieth time that day.

"Where is the canteen?" is the next question.

"Down at the far end of the waiting room, on the left," we reply, like a gramophone needle stuck in a groove, all the time carrying on with entries in the ledger, writing labels, making up mixtures, counting tablets, or hunting for the elusive eye drop bottle. If it happens to be towards the end of the afternoon, the patient is back within a few minutes, announcing with gloomy triumph, "The canteen is shut."

This is the last straw. We are tired, rushed off our feet, and submerged in scrips waiting to be done before five o'clock. We can only take a fresh grip on our professional civility and pray that we don't go straight up the wall.

If only Out Patients would remember to come provided with three or four separate shillings, in case of being given a multiple script by the doctor, and to bring back all bottles, jars, boxes and tablet phials which they have had on previous visits, they would find themselves greeted with a friendly smile through the hatch, instead of a weary and exasperated reception, which is entirely due to their own thoughtlessness.

We do manage to exchange friendly smiles through the hatch, strange as it may seem. One sweet old lady I remember in particular. It was in a hospital in a poor district of London. I took in a card which showed that the patient possessed the fascinating Christian name of Decima. I have known three sisters, cousins of my Mother, who were numbered off in their correct places in the family as Septima, Octavia and Nona, but the tally stopped there, and I had wondered at odd times what the next one would have been. I looked out and saw two dear old ladies standing outside, and I could not resist taking time off from the rat race, to speak to the owner of this charming name.

I made up the script, and as I handed it out I said, "Are you the youngest of the family?" She turned a pair of clear blue eyes, bright with surprise on me.

"No," she said, with a shy smile, "there's only Alice and me," indicating her companion. "Why do you ask"?

Because of your name," I replied, "it is so pretty and so unusual. Don't you know what it means?"

She shook her dear old head.

"I was called it after my mother," she said, "lots of people have told me what a pretty name it is, but I never knew it meant anything."

"It means the tenth child," I said. "I thought perhaps you were called that because you had nine older brothers and sisters."

The two old ladies beamed at me and each other.

"There Dessie," exclaimed the patient, "don't you remember our mother used to tell us of all her elder brothers and sisters? There was Uncle Joe and Auntie Lou and Uncle Henry and Aunt Eliza and Auntie Flo and Uncle Charlie - but there, we are wasting the lady's time."

She cut short the recital and turned to me. "Do you know, my dear," she said, with a charming old-fashioned grace," I shall be eighty four come next month, and Alice here will be eighty come January, and all our lives we have never known where my name came from, except it was my Mother's. We are never too old to learn, are we?"

And the two old sisters toddled off, arm in arm, whispering and twittering together like a couple of school girls, and probably spent the rest of the day counting up their long dead Victorian uncles and aunts to make quite sure their mother had been the tenth child.

Another numerical name I have come across is Penultima, and it is a tribute to the faith and self-confidence of the parents, that it proved to be a correct prophecy.

In another area there was an elderly gentleman who surname was Day. His initials were T.O. and I discovered that his names were - quite literally - Time Of. This had been a joke on the part of his father, but I am still wondering what the officiating clergyman had been thinking about to let the father get away with it at the Christening.

An Out Patients' Hall or Waiting Room has a sound all its own. As it comes to us in the pharmacy, it is like a feather bed about three feet thick, suspended horizontally in the air about a yard from floor level. It is composed of quietly chattering voices, the shuffling of many feet, the scraping of chair legs or creaking of benches, trolley wheels, doors opening and shutting, rustling of papers and magazines, and the occasional stretcher or bath chair. It is the most muffling and deadening noise imaginable, and it is almost impossible to distinguish any particular sound in the general miasma. The voices of small children and crying babies rise clearly above it, as they are on a much higher wave length. We have to call the patients' names when their medicines are ready, and trying to make oneself heard through this muffling layer of sound is a real strain on the voice. A male pharmacist can make himself heard without much trouble, as the masculine voice can batter its way through by sheer power; but a woman's voice comes exactly in the centre of the densest part of the layer, and a sore throat at the end of a busy day is quite a frequent occurrence.

My own voice is - as far as one can know one's own voice - of the quality usually described as high and light, and quite the most useless for making itself heard through the feather bed. I have taught myself however, by dint of long practice, to produce it so that it will come out - momentarily - with the low-pitched, penetrating resonance of a bronze gong. This slices below the level of the feather bed and hits everyone's eardrums with a reverberating clang, which invariably brings all heads round in astonishment. It is great fun suddenly producing my famous clarion note, and it is invaluable when calling the Out Patients.

Some O.Ps. have the irritating habit of standing outside the hatch after we have taken their card, thus getting in the way of others, and causing unnecessary delay. Delay is the one thing we cannot endure. In some hospitals the hatch is of ground glass, which makes this habit all the more annoying as we can see the shadowy outlines waiting impatiently, while we are running our feet off trying to catch up with the work. When they do this sort of thing, it gives me a fiendish joy to throw the hatch up quietly and do my Bull of Basham act close in their ears.

One day I got caught well and truly. Two vague figures had been standing at the hatch for some time, apparently immersed in a nice heart to heart chat. We were roaring busy, and I had had a particularly long and intricate card to work through. When I was ready I flung up the hatch, simultaneously letting out my deep-throated call for the patient in question. The two figures gave gasps of dismay and shot away in opposite directions as if I had dropped a grenade between them. They had the grace to look back with murmured apologies, but without stopping to glance at them I slammed down the hatch and grabbed the next script.

My colleague was quite a young girl, only recently qualified, and still new enough to be somewhat in awe of the medical staff. I found her gazing at me with round eyes. "Do you know who those were?" she asked in horrified tones.

"No", I replied, "and I don't care either. If there's one thing that sends me creeping up the ceiling, it's people gossiping outside the hatch when I'm busy."

"They were the Medical Superintendent and the Senior Consultant," she said, in a hushed voice of utter dismay, "and you shouted right in their ears and made them jump".

"Do them good," I retorted, "if it was the M.S. and Dr. Bingley they ought to know better than to do their consulting in Out Patients, leaning on my hatch. Teach them to do their dirty work in the proper place."

My little colleague stared at me aghast. Having generations of medical heredity behind me, I fear I have not quite the awe-stricken attitude towards the modern doctor that I might otherwise have.

The “reps” are a great feature in our lives. They are the kindly, helpful, knowledgeable men - and sometimes women - who travel round the country visiting both hospitals and retail chemists. They represent the manufacturing firms and research centres whence we obtain our stocks of drugs, dressings, instruments, gas cylinders and all the innumerable requisites. In time past they were known as "commercial travellers", then as "representatives" but now, briefly and affectionately, as "reps."

Nearly all reps employed by the big manufacturing firms of high repute, are qualified pharmacists. Many of them are research chemists and extremely well-informed and expert people. They can answer lucidly and unhesitatingly all our most searching technical questions about the new drugs and preparations and are an inexhaustible mine of information. They can give us full information upon the latest researches in the drug world; they keep us in touch with developments in every department of our work, and act as expert liaison officers throughout. Also, and this is a very important point to the busy pharmacist, they will always show the greatest consideration, and stand quietly aside when they see we are in a rush of work and wait till we are free to talk to them. This type of rep is always a welcome visitor to the pharmacy and ranks among the pharmacist's best friends.

They also act as unofficial employment agents. Frequently, when a rep has called and found me there on locum duty, he has immediately asked to take my name and address, in order to pass it on to some other hospital pharmacist in dire need of a locum, and I have picked up numerous excellent posts in this way. Their memory for faces is phenomenal. Over and over again when I have met a rep, if only for a few minutes, in some particular hospital, and then, months later, have met him again in another hospital in a totally different part of his territory, he has invariably recognised me. Very often he even remembers my name, but if that eludes him, he can unfailingly give the name of the hospital where we last met. It is absolutely uncanny.

Unfortunately, however, this helpful expert and delightful type of rep is outnumbered - though, I admit, not very heavily - by a very different type. This sort of pest invariably comes from some one-eyed firm or other and is merely trying to push some marvellous panacea for which he claims all the virtues of the Pharmacopoeia. He barges into the pharmacy on the crest of a flood of geniality, shakes hands enthusiastically all round, and immediately bursts into a non-stop flood of talk, quite regardless of whether we deal with his firm, or whether we are busy, or whether he is obviously unwelcome, in fact regardless of anything till he has got his parrot-learned sales talk off his chest. He is totally unable to answer any questions the least bit outside of what he has learned up, and to witness a wise and experienced pharmacist making mincemeat of this type, is a joy and an education.

This sort of rep has not the least concern with the fact that we are busy. He flings open his case, sprays the entire pharmacy with leaflets and pamphlets, distributes samples broadcast to everyone in sight, delivers a perfect spate of so called funny stories and jokes, and talks - and talks - and TALKS.

In my capacity of locum, I am in a strong position for dealing with them. One can sum up the type at a glance, and the name of their firm will tell the rest. All I do is to put on a frosty smile, say I am sorry but the regular pharmacist is on leave and I am only there on locum duty; and such being the case, I am quite unable to do anything for them. If they like to leave some literature and samples I will see that the pharmacist gets them on his return. Thank you so much. Good afternoon.

I never refuse samples, needless to say. At different times I have collected such tit-bits as hand cream, toothpaste, liniment guaranteed to ameliorate anything from a sprained thumb to lumbago, a smart plastic nail brush, tissues for cleaning spectacles, patent headache powders, and a particularly luscious sort of throat pastille. On my weekend visits home, my medicine cupboard becomes stacked with a truly amazing collection of oddments.

Quite recently I was doing duty at a hospital where I go regularly. I had met the regular pharmacist once or twice, though naturally I usually never meet the one for whom I am locum-ing. However, Mr. Patterson lived nearby, and was a pillar of the staff cricket club. When he was spending his leave at home, he would come in unofficially to deal with the serious business of cricket, and always paid me a friendly visit.

On this occasion he had been in for a chat and had then gone off on the real business of the day. A few moments later he came dashing back, his hair on end and his eyes popping.

"Where can I hide?" he gasped, looking wildly round the pharmacy, "I have just seen a rep in the front hall, and he is the world's bore. If he knows I am in the building he will keep me talking the rest of the afternoon."

"Behind that door," I exclaimed, "you'll have to sit on the autoclave. It's not turned on, only don't kick it for goodness sake, or the valves will rattle."

"Hold him off," he wailed, "don't give me away whatever you do. Tell him any lies you like." And he dived behind the door of the dressings cupboard on top of the autoclave. It was a mass of knobs and valves, so I hoped he was comfortable. The next moment the rep entered in full spate. I gave him a minute or two in which to blow off the worst of the pressure, or he would have burst a blood vessel, then said with a beautiful professional smile, "I am so sorry, but Mr. Patterson is on leave, and I am afraid I can't give you any orders in his absence."

Under my blandly fluting tones, and icy glance, his exuberance deflated quite pathetically. Out of the tail of my eye I could see the junior and the porter getting steadily redder and redder in the face with their efforts not to laugh, while all the time my ears were cocked for any betraying rattle from the autoclave.

It was a very meek rep who produced some pamphlets and samples and handed them to me.

"I will see that Mr. Patterson gets these as soon as possible," I said sweetly. "Thank you so much. Good afternoon."

The door had hardly closed behind him than there were a strangled explosion from Joe, a high-pitched squeal of joy from the junior, and Mr. Patterson was clasping me to his bosom.

"Oh! lovely, lovely!" he crooned. "I never thought you had it in you. That was the best bit of acting I ever saw in my life. And you got rid of him within five minutes! He usually stays for hours."

"And," I amended proudly, "I never told a single lie the whole way through

CHAPTER 7

In a great many cases the staff accommodation and food are much better in mental hospitals than in general hospitals. This is part of the drive to attract more young people to take up mental nursing. Also, despite the fact that our work in the pharmacy is quite as intensive in mental hospitals, the general atmosphere is more peaceful and relaxed.

Of course I know nothing of ward work, though we get echoes and repercussions of all the many and various crises which blow up at a moment's notice, especially in the Disturbed wards. But on the whole the tempo is geared to the slow movements of the patients, and a quiet and relaxed atmosphere is encouraged as much as possible. It is a most important part of the treatment for the patients that they should be allowed to go their own pace, without the ceaseless hustle and rush which is unavoidable in general work.

So far, in my experience, I have only found one mental hospital which can be classified as non-progressive, outdated and thoroughly bad.

I usually arrange my engagements so that I can be at home for a month or two during the winter, but one year I was inveigled into undertaking a three-month's locum, for November, December and January, at a certain mental hospital. I do not usually undertake anything longer than four weeks at a stretch at any one place, though I will always make return visits if required - and if I happen to like the place.

In this case, however, the Chief pharmacist had lost his assistant and was absolutely desperate for help. It is a very large hospital, and the work far too much for one person. The hospital was situated on the outskirts of a country town within easy reach of my home. It was too far to travel to and from home each day, but made my weekend visits home much easier than they usually are. It was for these reasons that I had agreed to do three months there, before my next season's round of engagements began.

Before I started on the job I went over one day to see the place. It was a typical mid-Victorian monstrosity in pseudo Byzantine style. The Chief pharmacist took me round. He was a quiet grey man, not much taller than myself though very strongly built. I found him curiously difficult to engage in conversation, though I can usually get back-chat out of a door post. He was not actually absent-minded, but I got the impression that it was something far deeper and more fundamental than that. We had the same feeling about the Medical Superintendent when we had met him at various lectures and gatherings before I took the post there. We did not know the M.S. at all well and had put it down to the mental abstraction of the great brain, but I realised that I was seeing exactly the same thing in the Chief pharmacist.

It was not absent-mindedness or mental abstraction! It was a deep and terrible paralysis of the soul. There was a miasma of evil over the whole place, as if decades of untold misery had soaked into the very soil and impregnated the whole atmosphere. I have never known any place with such a terrible influence. As I came to know many members of the staff, I recognised that ghastly condition over and over again. It was not mental; it was as if the very soul were trapped and suffocated in some unseen place of horror.

The hospital itself was no better, and very little worse, than other mental hospitals. As Mr. Thorpe took me round I noticed that some of the enclosures were still surrounded by the high, incurved iron railings, but they were in the process of being removed, and the grounds and gardens were well tended.

The pharmacy was extremely good, spacious and well arranged, and meticulously neat and tidy. It was not quite as super as the pharmacy where I had worked with Tiny and Ernst, but it ran a good second. Mr.

Thorpe was one of the tidiest and most neat fingered people I have ever worked with, though not in the least pernickety or fussy.

When I arrived to commence duty a few days later Mr. Thorpe met me in his car and drove me to the Nurses' Home, which I had only seen in the distance on my first visit. It was an enormous old seventeenth century mansion, standing in the grounds nearly half a mile from the hospital. In its prime it must have been a magnificent place, but now it was a hollow, ghostly shell. The huge entrance hall and wide staircase were shabby and neglected, and the lovely old cornices and ceilings were blackened and hung with cobwebs. The great drawing room still showed the beautiful Georgian wall panels, but they and the paint work were stained and peeling. This room was used for the staff recreation room, and the worn shabby furniture was dwarfed into meanness and insignificance by the lovely proportions of the architecture. Everywhere was decay and desolation.

I never saw the main part of the first floor at all, though I gathered that all the great bedrooms had been divided into cubicles like horse boxes. My bedroom was in what had been the servants' quarters, at the top of the back stairs. These led up from a side entrance, through stone flagged passages, and past a perfect rabbit warren of dark and dismal rooms, which must originally have been larders, pantries and store rooms. Some were roughly fitted up with rows of wash basins and pegs for the use of the nurses, but the plaster was coming off in patches all over the place, the paint work was dingy and battered, and the ceilings black and filthy. The back stairs were narrow and uncarpeted, and led up into a labyrinth of dark narrow passages.

When I was shown into my room, I involuntary stopped short in dismay, for it was the dreariest and most forbidding room I had ever been expected to occupy. Mr. Thorpe had kindly carried my cases up for me, and I caught his eyes fixed on me in desperate anxiety lest I should refuse to stay and decide to go straight home again. It was only the unconscious appeal that I saw in his face that decided me to stay and at least give the job a try out.

The bedroom was a long narrow slice taken off an originally larger room. The ceiling was very high, dark and grimy. The one tall window looked out over a dreary stone paved yard, with overhanging trees and a general atmosphere of damp, moss grown dankness. The walls and paint work were a dingy yellow, and the one centre light, shadeless and feeble, showed the wallpaper torn away in great patches, behind which the plaster was crumbling and flaking away. The curtains and bed cover were faded and torn, there was no wash basin, no bedside light, and no fire, either gas or electric. There was an armchair, so called, with the upholstery in holes and the springs broken and sagging. When I came to examine the bed, I found the mattress was flock, as old as the hills, and one mass of lumps. The pillows were obviously some that had been used for the patients in the bad old days, and which should have been condemned and burned years ago. The bedstead was of the iron frame type, with springs sagged down into a trough through decades of wear. There was a couple of mats on the floor, but they were torn and scuffed; the linoleum was in shreds. And over all, permeating the very air, was that feeling of psychic gloom and horror which chilled my very soul.

I have had to stay in many rooms of varying degrees of discomfort at one time and another, but invariably I have been able to impose my own personality in a very short time, and though not always able to alter the actual contents of the room, at least to introduce an atmosphere of comfort and life. But I could do nothing with this room. That underlying, all pervading, overpowering atmosphere of misery and haunted gloom filled every corner of the old house. It was perceptible everywhere in the hospital, in the gardens and in the woodlands, but most of all it was concentrated in that old house. I fought it the whole time I was there. I told myself it was pure imagination, that I was letting the physical discomforts get me down, that I was being a fool, and that I would not - repeat not - let myself be overcome by it. But to no avail.

I started off by determining that I would get a bit of comfort and vitality into my bedroom. In any case I was furious at being provided with such disgraceful accommodation and immediately I had finished making a thorough investigation I got on the inter-phone to the M.S. and blew my top well and truly. It was no business of his, but I was too angry to care. He was utterly dismayed and genuinely distressed, as I reeled off my tale of complaints. The sagging bed - the thin lumpy mattress - the straw pillows - the wretched blankets - the broken-down armchair - the worn and dirty mats - I spared him nothing.

When I returned from the pharmacy the following evening, I was met by a wide-eyed maid.

"Oo-er," she said, "we ain't 'arf 'ad an 'ow-d'ye-do over your room today. 'Is Nibs 'as bin over 'ere, and Matron and all the lot of 'em one after another. First off we 'as to fetch out a new bed, and no sooner 'ave I got that made up, but along they comes from Stores with one of them new internal mattresses, and I 'as to strip it off and make it up all over again. I just got that done, when along they comes again with new blankets and pillers and rugs and what-all, and I 'as to do the bed a third time. I just got the room straight when over they comes and takes out that there old broken down chair, and puts you in a couple o' nice ones what they fetched out o' the doctors' quarters. Oo, we ain't 'arf 'ad a day, I can tell yer."

I went round the room examining everything, while she stood and watched my every movement. Certainly, there was an enormous improvement. The rattling old iron bedstead had been replaced by a very good, new, divan bed, the mattress was an excellent interior sprung, the blankets clean and new, and the pillows soft and good. Daphne kept up a running commentary as she watched me.

"I 'ad to make up that room before you come," she said, "and as I was doin' it I thinks to myself, I thinks, now what sort of a person are they 'avin in 'ere I should like to know. Can't be anybody much, or they wouldn't 'ave the nerve to put all this old rubbish in 'ere, I thinks. Then when I sees you last night, I thinks, she won't stick that sort o' thing long. Either she'll walk right out, or she'll raise 'ell. Then when I sees you wasn't walkin' straight out last night, I thinks to myself, oo-er, Daph, you're for it. She's goin' to raise 'ell sure as eggs. But I'm glad you did," she added generously, "we could do with a few more like you round 'ere. Someone as'll speak out and stand up for themselves."

"Who is supposed to be in charge here?" I asked. "Isn't there a Home Sister or Warden or someone responsible for the Nurses' Home?"

"Nah," she replied, contemptuously, "they don't go in for nothin' o' that 'ere. Now in other 'ospitals where I've worked, we 'ad a proper 'Ome Sister, or a Warden, like you says, someone as could be in charge like, and keep a eye on things. But they don't 'ave nothin' o' that 'ere."

"Well, who do I ask if I want anything?" I said. "Supposing I wanted a new globe in the light, or anything of that sort? Isn't there anyone in charge at all?"

"There's only Edna in the canteen," she replied, "but she ain't supposed to 'ave nothin' to do with upstairs. By rights Miss Dalton's supposed to look after the place, but she never puts 'er nose near. She's too busy runnin' round after Matron, makin' up to 'er and creepin' round 'er. Proper snake she is, ever ser nice to 'er face, an' tearin' 'er to pieces be'ind 'er back."

"Miss Dalton is the Assistant Matron, isn't she?" I asked.

"Yus," said Daphne, "an' she's some Assistant, I don't think."

This conversation was very illuminating. I do not make a habit of getting information from maids, but there seemed to be an unspoken covenant of silence throughout the whole staff. Everyone knew that the Administration was in a disgraceful state, that the whole place was a seething mass of laziness, shirking, incompetence, self-seeking, job-snatching inefficiency, yet not one single person had the courage to stand up to the Heads of Departments and report anything.

The Medical Superintendent, the Matron, the hospital Secretary and Finance Officer apparently thought the place was being excellently run, and they and the Management Committee formed a close combine. They presented a face of shining complacence to the public, assured everyone that the hospital was one big happy family, but never once did any one of them emerge from their ivory tower and get down into the departments and investigate matters for themselves. Each one was so surrounded by sycophants and yes-men that not one had the slightest idea of the real condition of things, and couldn't care less, as long as they themselves were not bothered.

This is one infallible indication which I have observed in my travels, which tells immediately if the administration is good, and if the heads of departments are doing their jobs efficiently. It is very simple, but gives the show away every time.

If the Big Four, that is, the Matron, the M.S., the secretary and the finance officer, take their midday meal in the open dining room, along with the rest of the staff, one can rest assured that they know their job, and are doing it to the best of their ability. The hospital may not be top grade, and there are invariably faults and discrepancies in every large community, but as a general rule this never fails. If the staff, right through to the ward maids, laundry women and porters, see that the Medical Superintendent - Poppa - 'Is Nibs - The Old Man - Father - or even 'Is Whiskers - for the M.S. has dozens of appellations behind his back - is having exactly the same meals as they are, carrying his own tray, taking his own utensils back to the service hatch, exactly like everybody else, it immediately gives them a sense of security and unity, in a way in which nothing else can.

They would die sooner than express any appreciation of course, and the word "loyal" is far too out-moded ever to enter their heads. But the occasional remark, and the whole atmosphere of the hospital, show that the loyalty is there, consciously or not.

"Bumped right into old Whiskers with me tray 'smornin', comin' round from the 'atch. Nearly sent 'is jelly flyin'".

"Coo; bet 'e looked at you a bit old-fashioned. Did 'e say anythink?"

"Yus. Begged me pardon, and said it was 'is fault civil as you please. 'E ain't a bad old stick, not like some as I could name. I'd take a lot from 'im what I wouldn't from other folks."

That is genuine loyalty, as true and deep as any that might be decked out with bunting and elegant phraseology.

In a number of hospitals which I know, it is quite the usual thing, when standing in the queue at the serving counter, to see the M.S. a few yards away, next to a group of giggling ward maids. Further back, down the corridor, can be seen the secretary, gossiping with the hall porter, or the telephonist, and at the far end of the queue a group of white-coated doctors deep in conversation with the librarian and the assistant physiotherapist.

This is the atmosphere which makes a hospital tick over on oiled wheels. The senior staff know how to keep their authority, yet at the same time they can mix effortlessly with every other member of the staff, whatever their position.

In other hospitals the atmosphere is not quite as democratic, and the different departments tend to hang together at meal times. But even so, there mere fact that the Heads are taking their meals in the common dining room gives a feeling of good fellowship, besides which the fact that the M.S. or one of the other V.I.P.s may be next in line to be served, keeps the catering and dining room staff on their toes, and goes far to ensure that both the food and the service is up to scratch.

But not in this hospital. Nothing of the sort. The heads of departments were far too careful of their own little dignity ever to be seen taking their meals in the general dining room. They had to have theirs served in some rarefied fastness of their own.

Even at the staff dances and socials, and above all at the big Christmas party and dance for the staff and all such patients as were capable of joining in, the M.S. and his wife, the Matron and her shadow Miss Dalton, the secretary and the finance officer, invariably made up a tight little clique of their own. They had a table to themselves at the top of the Hall and were never known to speak a single word to anyone. At the dances they would put in a gracious appearance, partner each other for a few dances, then disappear, leaving the rest of the rabble to get on with it. Not one of them ever danced with anyone outside their own clique. Having known the M.S. and his wife quite apart from the hospital world, I might have expected to be included in their party, or at least to have been asked for a dance. But that would have put too much of a strain on their precariously balanced pedestals. I was not in the least desirous of being included in their clique. I had my own circle of friends among the junior medical staff, the occupational therapists, the stenographers, the senior Charge Nurses, and some of the younger and more outgoing of the Sisters. We always got together at these functions and enjoyed ourselves enormously. We usually contrived, deliberately, to get a large table in a position where the high and mighties could see and hear our vulgar and uproarious goings on, and whence we could watch their obvious embarrassment and self-conscious looks.

Not one of them ever seemed at ease in the presence of the rest of the staff, and were totally unable to relax or unbend, for fear of jeopardising their dignity. The natural result was that they were intensely disliked and jeered at bitterly and unmercifully behind their backs.

One after another I crossed swords with every head of department in turn, from the M.S. downwards, till my name stank throughout the whole Admin: Staff. To give them their due, every time I took a complaint to any head of department I was treated with the utmost civility, even with agitated concern, and they immediately fell over themselves to give me any mortal thing I wanted, just as had happened on my very first day, when I complained to the M.S. about my bedroom.

The holes in the wall paper, the crumbling plaster got on my nerves to such an extent that I had the bright idea of buying a number of railway posters, which I fixed with drawing pins over the worst of the holes. When framed with passe-partout tape they certainly went far towards enlivening the room. But they cost quite a bit, and I did not see why I should make improvements to my shoddy accommodation at my own expense. So before ordering them, I went along to the finance officer, told him my room was in a disgraceful state, and that I proposed getting some posters, as much to cheer up the room, as to prevent plaster falling down my neck in bed, and what about it?

He was apparently shaken to the core on hearing that my room was in such a state of disrepair, and immediately took time off to go across to the old house and see for himself. Having done so, he came to me, all apologies, told me to buy as many posters as I liked, and to send the receipt in to Finance when it would be refunded to me. I did so and sat back and waited for the refund.

I waited for weeks, and still no sign of that refund. I simmered for a bit longer, then suddenly blew up. By then I had been there long enough to have acquired a very good idea of the rottenness which permeated the whole Admin: Staff. I knew the filthiness of the food, and the utter disregard for the most elementary consideration for the welfare of the staff, and I had become acquainted with the hypocrisy and back biting which surged through every department. Also, I was in a very strong position. All the senior staff had been there for many years and had had no experience of any other hospital. The heads of the departments were far too comfortably bedded in their jobs to wish to break down the wall of adulation and "yes sir" which they had built up around themselves. That terrible atmosphere of depression and inertia, combined with the determination of the departmental staff that their heads should be kept in cosy ignorance, sapped and stifled the attempts of any subordinates who might wish to approach them.

I had come in like a comet from outer space, and I had behind me the experience of a large number of up-to-date and progressive hospitals. Also, I knew that my job was of vital importance and that it would be almost impossible to replace me - as they all very well knew - besides which I had a husband and a home behind me. I was not dependant on the job, I was not tied by the hopes of a pension as were so many of the Sisters, and in any case, I have always enjoyed a good fight in the cause of justice. I am a long-suffering soul in the ordinary way, and by no means a deliberate trouble maker, but there was something in the bland, self-satisfied hypocrisy of the whole set up, that got clean up my nose. I waited till I came nicely to boiling point, then blew my top.

Marching in through the outer office, I brushed aside all the clerks who frantically tried to intercept me and knocked on the great man's door; acutely aware of the dismay I left in my wake.

I started off by saying that I had never received the refund for the posters which I had been promised weeks before. Having warmed up nicely on that theme, I then proceeded to tell him his hospital was a perfect disgrace, the staff meals were a scandal, the accommodation atrocious, and the general administration the worst I had come across in all my experience. I topped off by saying that if it were not that the job suited my own convenience, and out of consideration for Mr. Thorpe, I should leave tomorrow.

The wretched man was completely dumbfounded. His nice little ivory castle was being dynamited about his ears by a simply unspeakable female who had not the slightest respect for him, or his more than thirty years in the place, or his carefully nurtured self-esteem. He had not a word to say in reply to my observations, but rang at once for his chief clerk, and proceeded to give him a most humiliating ticking off for not having paid me the refund; ordering him to produce it immediately. I knew, and we each knew that the other knew, that the old so-and-so had never said a word to him about it and was merely putting the blame on him in order to save his own face.

I pocketed the money, and as I went out through the outer office I winked at the chief clerk to show there was no personal animosity intended, but ever after when I want to the office for my salary, I was accorded the sort of reception which might have been given to a walking crate of gelignite.

The food was truly appalling. One does not expect delicacies in hospital fare, but one does at least expect it to be wholesome and eatable. We came to the conclusion that the authorities must have bought up an enormous consignment of tinned tomatoes cheap. We had squashy, watery tinned tomatoes morning, noon and night the whole time I was there. I had my breakfast in my room, also my supper; and these meals were prepared in the Canteen at the Nurses' Home. Day after day, week in, week out, these revolting tinned tomatoes appeared in a swimming mess on my tray. Sometimes bits of over cooked bacon or fried bread were floating in it, occasionally a broken fried egg or scorched sausage would be there, but whatever it was, was invariably soggy and swimming in watery tomato juice. The tinned tomatoes were of the poorest quality too, flavourless and nauseating.

My midday dinner I had in a small private dining room, in the main building. It was supposed to be a great favour and concession, not to say an honour, for me to use the private dining room, but even so the food was usually uneatable. It was either scorched and dried all-round the edge of the plate, or else the vegetables were half raw, and the meat invariably tough. I shared the dining room with the Occupational Therapist, whom I came to know as Catherine.

CHAPTER 8

Catherine was a thin, grey-haired, frail little creature, not much older than myself, but looking a good ten or fifteen years more than her age. She had been there many years and was all but broken in health and spirit by the evil atmosphere, and the utter lack of any interest or co-operation in her work shown to her by the authorities. In all mental hospitals with any pretensions to a modern outlook or progressive methods, occupational therapy is regarded as only second in importance to the actual medical treatment. The Occupational Therapy department is one of very great importance, and the chief therapist is given every encouragement and assistance.

But not so here. Oh, no.

Instead of being given promising patients who could derive real benefit from the O.T. Catherine was given the most hopeless and retarded types, who were no good for laundry, or scrubbing or scullery work. If a patient made a nuisance of herself on the ward, she was sent to O.T. to get her out of the way. This of course, gave the patients the impression that O.T. was a form of punishment, and this made them even more sullen, non-co-operative and difficult than they normally were.

I conceived the greatest admiration for Catherine. Year after year she struggled on in her work, doing her absolute utmost for the patients, teaching, coaxing, encouraging from morning to night. She also organised all the Fancy Dress Dances for them, the little concerts and entertainments, the singing classes and the Church choir. She was organist, accompanist, producer, wardrobe mistress, make-up artist, and even made time to write little plays suited to the patients' acting abilities.

And never once did she get a word of appreciation or encouragement from the top level.

Catherine had a bed-sitting room in the servants' wing of the old house, near my room. It was certainly much larger than mine, and she had her own furniture and possessions which made it quite civilised and pleasant; but even so there was no getting away from the gloom with which that place was saturated. I spent many of my evenings with her, smoking and gossiping, helping her to string bead necklaces for the Fancy Dress Dance, stitching bits of gaudy finery, or helping to mend the sadly worn dresses from the acting wardrobe. During those evenings I could see only too clearly the toll that place had taken of her. Many a time she was so utterly worn out that she fell asleep even as we talked.

Some years previously she had a severe nervous breakdown, and acute gastric trouble, directly due to overwork and bad living conditions. But she dared not leave or try to seek other work. She had another two or three years to go before she arrived at pensionable age, and she was holding on desperately for the sake of the pension. Also, she had a deep love for the patients, and was about the only person in the whole place who took a warm and personal interest in their welfare.

Catherine was supposed to be on a special gastric diet, and the authorities knew this perfectly well. In theory she was supplied with the correct diet, but the result in practise was truly deplorable. Over and over again when we sat down to our midday meal - the main meal of the day - all that was put before her was a minute portion of coarse fish, which had been boiled early in the day and kept hot, till it had dried and shrivelled to the consistency and appearance of leather. No sauce or any form of garnishing was ever supplied, and it was usually accompanied by watery boiled potatoes, lumpy tapioca or bright pink blancmange. My meals were not much better, but I did at least get some form of meat and vegetables, however badly cooked or served, but I have often seen Catherine hold her handkerchief over her mouth and turn away shuddering, as she struggled to control her retching stomach. Often tears of sheer hunger and disgust came to her eyes, as the nauseating mess appeared on the table.

The Catering Officer was not to blame. He had come a few years before, young, highly trained and enthusiastic, and had done his utmost to improve the meals for the staff and patients alike. But like everyone else, he had come up against the stone wall of inertia and lack of support from the top level, which was reflected in the indifference and couldn't care less attitude of his subordinates. His health was beginning to break down under the strain, and he left while I was there.

Having come to logger-heads with the M.S. over my room on my arrival, and with the finance officer later on, I raised Cain with the secretary over the meals.

One day, when a more than usually badly cooked and unappetising meal appeared, I leapt up from the table, stormed across to his office, and demanded that he should come immediately and see for himself the sort of filth that we were expected to eat. I told Catherine to stay and keep watch that it was not whisked away, and something better substituted before I got back.

The secretary was as utterly dumbfounded at my attack, as the finance officer had been, and of course immediately tried to pass the buck. Quite possibly he was quite correct in saying that he was not the person responsible, but I was past caring. I was determined to raise the dust with someone in authority, and I didn't care two pence on whose head it fell. He stuttered and puffed and blew, while I got it off my chest, then fled to his car, muttering that he would have the matter looked into, and made his escape to his own home where - judging by his rotund and well upholstered contours - he probably had a delicious chicken lunch awaiting him.

Later that afternoon Mr. Thorpe, glancing out of the pharmacy windows which overlooked the front entrance, remarked "What's going on out here?"

I peered over his shoulder and saw the secretary, the catering officer and the chef, in a close huddle on the drive at the foot of the main steps. There seemed to be a certain amount of tenseness in the atmosphere. I had not said anything to Mr. Thorpe about my lunch time interview with the secretary, but by the actions and expressions of the group I could make a very good guess as to the subject under discussion.

"Go on," I said, "go down into the stockroom and stand by the little window in the oxygen store. See if you can hear what it is all about."

He threw me a glance of the deepest suspicion. Of course, my escapades with the M.S. and the finance officer had long been hospital property, and the dear little man was inclined to regard his assistant with great wariness. The grin all over my face did nothing to reassure him.

"That would be eavesdropping", he protested, though quite without conviction, for I was already getting him stimulated to quite a degree of vivacity, and he was even occasionally exhibiting the resuscitation of a long dormant sense of humour.

"Nonsense," I retorted, "go on, hurry up or you'll miss the fun," and I hustled him down the cellar stair.

Presently he came back, lugging a heavy oxygen cylinder.

"What's that for?" I demanded.

"Well," he replied sheepishly, "if you will drive me down to the gas store to eavesdrop, I must at least pretend I went down for the proper purpose."

"You and your conscience," I jeered, "it will be the death of you if you don't get the better of it. Did you make out what the huddle is about?"

He carefully propped the cylinder in a corner remarking that Ted could take it back when he came in, then turned to me with a look of profound reproach.

"What have you been doing now?" he asked. "I couldn't hear much of what was going on, but I gathered the secretary was putting the catering officer and the chef though the hoop properly, and I heard your name mentioned several times. Don't tell me you have been getting across the secretary this time."

I proceeded to tell him all about it, while he stared at me, solemn and wide eyed.

"It doesn't do any good losing your temper," he observed mildly when I had finished.

"Possibly not," I retorted, "but it doesn't half release my inhibitions."

"Inhibitions!" he echoed, "I shouldn't have thought you even knew the meaning of the word. I have never known anyone like you. You don't seem to care what you say to anybody, no matter who."

"I don't," I replied, "at least not when there's anything that needs saying. And there is plenty that needs saying around this place, as you ought to know after all the years you've been here."

He nodded sadly, remarking, "I wish there were a few more like you around," and proceeded to immerse himself in his ledgers.

From then on there was a revolution in the catering. I never heard another word from a soul, but the food improved out of all knowledge. Apart from that, the only repercussions were the murderous glances turned on me by the kitchen and dining.room staff, but that did not worry me in the least. I had achieved my object, Catherine was getting food which she could eat with reasonable enjoyment, and though we still had to work through the remainder of the consignment of tinned tomatoes in the Nurses' Home, the midday meals at the hospital were quite unrecognisable.

It was not only in the buildings that the atmosphere of oppression and evil was so potent, nor was it entirely due to the bad administration and the ill feeling which was rife among the personnel.

The Nurses' Home stood about half a mile away from the main hospital, and that walk through the grounds was the most eerie and terrifying I have ever known. Being there in the winter, it was usually pitch dark by the time I came off duty at five o'clock. The path ran alongside the hospital and outbuildings for a hundred yards or so, and this part was fitted with outside lights. From then on, beyond the group of staff garages, the road abruptly deteriorated into a gravel track and the lights ceased. On one side was rough undergrowth and tall trees, but on the other was a series of compounds, surrounded by towering yews. These compounds were the old burial grounds of the hospital. Some had been levelled and turfed, but there was one which was in occasional use. It was sordid, weed grown and utterly dreary, the pathetic little pauper memorials of cast iron all askew among the brambles and nettles, and the graves uncared for, untended and forgotten.

At one time I should have been far too terrified to walk down that dark path alone, past those graveyards, and even so it took every ounce of mental control to make myself walk without hurrying and without looking over my shoulder at every step. I deliberately made myself walk more slowly than usual, in order to ensure that my mind was in full control of the terrors which might so easily have leapt upon me.

Beyond the burial enclosures began a patch of thick woodland, and here the track was no more than a narrow, muddy footpath. I had to use a torch, otherwise I would have missed the path and wandered, lost, among the trees and undergrowth, for it was entirely unlighted right up to the drive of the old house. There was no other way, except by leaving the hospital grounds and going right round by the main road, which more than doubled the distance. As the patients were allowed to roam freely about the grounds, it did not in any way add to one's peace of mind to know that at any moment one might bump into an unstable mental type in those dark woods. All the young nurses, girls and men, used that path, and apparently thought nothing of it, but they always traversed it in chattering groups, which was rather a different matter from doing it alone.

Depressing and eerie though the path was, the deep aura of evil seemed to intensify in the vicinity of the old house. For a long time, I would not believe my senses, but then I found I was not the only one who was aware of it.

Eleanor was the junior Registrar, a tall graceful creature who became, and has remained, a great friend of mine. She was not much younger than myself, having commenced her study of medicine at a much later age than is usual. She had what was politely described as a flat in the doctors' quarters in the old house, but which merely consisted of one enormous, bleak room, with a small shabby bathroom alongside. It had a fireplace, but the maids were far too lazy to see that there was a decent fire there when she came back from her rounds of the wards. Night after night she would come in, shivering with cold, to find the fireplace banked up with a black mass of coal dust, from which a feeble trickle of smoke was rising, sometimes up the chimney, but more often out into the room, which was like a mausoleum. When I was not sitting with Catherine, I spent most of my evenings with Eleanor, in fact as time went on I was more frequently with her than with Catherine, for the latter, on top of her days work, gave up most of her evenings to choir practises or rehearsals for the Christmas tableaux.

Eleanor and I would huddle together over the miserable fire, wrapped in rugs and blankets, sharing cigarettes and biscuits, and indulge in endless discussions about the general set-up of the hospital.

One evening she said, "Do you notice anything queer about this place! I mean apart from the mismanagement and the disgraceful administration?"

"Oh, you feel it too, do you?" I said. "I am thankful to find someone else who does, as I was beginning to think I was going psychotic or something."

Thence forward we discussed the matter from every possible angle but could find nothing definite to account for it. But if ever a place were haunted, that old house was.

Eleanor loved coming into the pharmacy, which she declared was the only place in the hospital where there was a bit of sane and wholesome fun to be found. She said most of the medical staff were going mental, and from what I saw of them I could well believe it. She and I fooled about and ragged and teased Mr. Thorpe till the dear little man didn't know if he was coming or going. He had cheered up in the most remarkable manner, and Catherine, who had known him for many years, said he was a different creature since I had come to work there.

One day, when my time of departure was drawing near, Eleanor was in the pharmacy, and asked Mr. Thorpe if he had anyone in prospect to take my place. I could not stay beyond my appointed date, as I had other engagements ahead.

"No," he said sadly, "I have asked the Committee about it over and over again, but they haven't done a thing about getting anyone else, not even put an advert in the Journal."

"That's just like them," Eleanor raged, "they will let you work yourself to death or dementia sooner than lift a finger about it."

That hospital was so back-dated that the wards were still under the bad old systems of numbers, instead of the now almost universal system of names. For some reason or other, when wards are numbered, the number is never used in the singular, but always in the plural. The admission ward happened to be number five, where the new intakes were put on arrival, but it was invariably known as "Fives."

As Eleanor spoke, an absurd doggerel suddenly formed in my mind, and I tap danced - an achievement of many years ago - the length of the pharmacy, chanting,

"He'll hang by his toes from the ceiling,

"T'will be marvel if he survives,

So we'll scoop him up in a butterfly net,

And carry him down to Fives."

Eleanor immediately took it up, and seizing me in her arm's the Registrar and the Assistant Pharmacist waltzed round and round the pharmacy, singing our extempore war song, while Mr. Thorpe and Ted gaped at us open mouthed.

Yes, we certainly livened up Mr. Thorpe and his pharmacy between us.

Another cheerful visitor was an elderly man who was Chief Mortuary Attendant. He was a fine old chap, and ex-Guardsman, and he came in every morning for a few minutes to have his coffee and biscuits with us. He was always immaculately neat and smart, and had a perfect fund of stories, all of them with a distinctly macabre slant, as was only to be expected from the nature of his occupation. Mr. Thorpe always kept a worried eye on me during these reminiscences and recitals and would surreptitiously hush up the cheery Mr. Hardy when he thought the yarns were becoming too spicy for my delicate ears.

But he need not have worried. One of the odd posts I held for a time during the war, was that of secretary receptionist to an undertaker, and the yarns I heard in that office would have put a perm in a donkey's tail. All undertakers and mortuary attendants when off duty, are the most sprightly and cheerful souls, bursting with humour and bonhomie; and if their style of humour is not suited to the squeamish - well the only way out is to get another job. This is not callousness of lack of sympathetic feeling on their part. It is purely a defence mechanism against the dreariness and often gruesomeness of their calling. But the joviality is never forced. It is only those who have a natural fund of cheeriness and gaiety who can stand up to the life, and the moment they are off duty all their natural good spirits come bubbling up to the surface. The men thoroughly enjoyed what they called a "topper and tails" funeral, and all, especially the older ones, who could remember when funerals really were funerals, with full panoply of black horses, crape hat bands, and even the huge black feather affairs which used to be placed on the corners of the hearses, were inclined to despise the quiet "car and crem:" type which is becoming increasingly prevalent, and which they found boring. The older men, who had known these early glories, would keep the younger men, and myself open mouthed for hours, as they recited their memories of past grandeur. I would help them into their black coats, brush them down, polish their top hats, and watch them settle their cheery faces into the appropriate expression of sedate gloom. On their return off would come the black coats and hats, which I had to replace carefully in the big store cupboards, and then we would settle down to a nice cup of tea, while they regaled me with all the fascinating details.

Dear Mr. Thorpe would have been shocked to the core if he had known all this. He was a gentle, sensitive soul, with an old-fashioned, chivalrous attitude to women, which I found very touching. He would never have believed that I was far tougher and more hard boiled than he would ever know how to be.

I found Mr. Hardy's stories extremely interesting from the physiological point of view, far more than from the purely sensational. Both he and Mr. Thorpe had known all the patients for years, and often it was only at the autopsy that the true nature of the complaint was fully revealed. Mr. Thorpe was also interested from this standpoint, but he could never understand that I felt the same about it, and he would usually take Mr. Hardy off into the store room to finish their coffee, just when the recital was reaching the most interesting point, much to my disappointment, though I appreciated the action to the full.

CHAPTER 9

In spite of - in fact very largely because of - our miseries and discomforts, half a dozen of us coalesced into a close-knit little gang, determined to have what fun we could. Catherine, Eleanor and myself formed the nucleus, and the others were two or three young women doctors. All of us except Catherine, had come to the hospital within a few weeks of each other, and one by one got drawn into our party. We spent our evenings in each other's rooms and put in hours of talk, wherein we pulled the hospital to pieces, put it together again, slanged all the heads of departments, tore strips off the senior medical staff, and generally got down to the serious business of resolving our inhibitions.

Eleanor's room was the most convenient meeting place, and we sat on the floor - having first carefully blocked the draughts which howled under the doors - sprawled on the chairs and on the bed, all of which were usually deep in Eleanor's study books, case sheets, medical literature, half empty boxes of chocolates, letters and banana skins, for Eleanor was one of the most untidy people I have ever met.

My room was hopeless as a meeting place. The doctors' rooms were far better than mine, though they were all cold, bleak and comfortless as each other. When Eleanor first saw my room, she gazed round in horror.

"I could never stop in a place like this," she exclaimed, "it would give me the creeps. It is just like a coffin, deep and long and narrow."

"For goodness sake don't put such ideas into my head," I expostulated, "it is all I can do to endure it in any case, and if you start giving me the heebie-jeebies I shall go clean bats. You should have seen it when I first came, it is a palace now by comparison."

"I don't know how you exist," she said, "you haven't even got a fire."

There were pipes running through the room, with an enormous old black radiator; but there was no means of controlling the heat. Sometimes during the night, the pipes got so hot that I was nearly stifled, and at other times I would come in from work, perished with cold, to find the pipes and radiator icy, and the room like a fridge. As I feel extremes of temperature acutely, this was one of my greatest penances. I know of nothing more utterly annihilating than to be cold and have no means of getting warm. I can endure bad food, and quite a lot of other discomforts with a fair amount of equanimity, but cold makes me feel thoroughly ill. No amount of thick clothing makes the slightest difference. If I am cold I remain cold, no matter how much I wrap up, and only some extraneous form of heat, such as a fire or a hot water bottle, will warm me up. But there was nowhere even to boil a kettle, unless one braved the stone corridors and arctic winds of the old sculleries downstairs. By the time one had been down and stood and waited for the kettle to boil on the battered old gas stove, one's last state was worse than the first.

The approach of Christmas brought a glow of happiness even to that haunted and hag-ridden place. Catherine spent most of her free time in rehearsing the patients for the Tableaux, and when she and I got most of the costumes mended, and the jewellery and finery in more or less working order, I helped her with the rehearsals. I have never had any experience in amateur theatricals since one occasion when I was at school, and was hauled in, under loud protest, and made to take the part of an Indian water carrier. My utter disgust at having my skin smeared with dark coloured make-up, and my long fair hair carefully screwed up under a tawdry turban, was only matched by the giggles caused by the appearance of my blue eyes staring furiously out of my darkened face. Since then I have eschewed amateur theatricals.

Catherine, on the other hand, was highly experienced at this sort of thing. She had done a great deal in first class amateur performances in her earlier years and had organised the patients' tableaux ever since she had been at the hospital.

The show was not, strictly speaking, planned as tableaux, for there was to be movement and action though without any spoken parts. It was quite hard enough to teach the patients their simple actions, without attempting the hopeless task of trying to teach them any words. It took every ounce of our energy and "give" to get any sort of order into things. The patients would stand round, helpless and dumb, while we pulled, pushed, prodded and cajoled till we were nearly exhausted. Then having got one or two of the chief performers in a scene in more or less their right places, on looking round we would find that Melchior and the Third Shepherd had sloped off to have a smoke behind the furnace room, while the Leading Angel and St. Joseph were indulging in a tickle and slap session in the ward kitchen on Threes.

Catherine was used to this sort of thing, but between helpless spasms of laughter, and attacks of hair tearing exasperation, I often felt I was going as crackers as the patients.

Catherine knew all the patients personally and was well acquainted with all their little ways. She had also written in a number of extra parts in the Bible scenes in order to give opportunity of including as many of them as possible.

The high spot of the performance was to be the scene depicting the presentation of gifts by the Magi. Catherine and I had spent many evenings concocting wonderful objects to represent the Gold, Frankincense and Myrrh. I considered the offering of Gold as a really classy effort on my part. The base consisted of an old bread board which Ted had scrounged for me from somewhere. On this I had fixed, by means of tacks through their bases, a number of tins and boxes from the pharmacy rubbish bins. An overall coating of gold paint made a most impressive offering. Its great advantage was the fact that it would not break if dropped or even if subjected to fairly rough handling, for old Arthur, who was to play the part of Caspar and present the gift, was notoriously erratic in his moods and actions. If he suddenly took the fit he had a habit of throwing anything available at the nearest person's head, so we didn't want to take unnecessary risks. With Mr. Thorpe's help I had fixed that golden gift so that it was guaranteed to withstand any amount of throwing about, though we could not guarantee the same for any head it might happen to hit.

The substance of the gifts depended very largely upon the person who was to carry them. The part of Melchior was taken by a much younger man, Ronnie. He was a very intelligent type, but schizophrenic, and had held a good position in a glass manufacturing firm. He was an absolute authority on glassware, both modern and antique, and could be relied upon implicitly when it came to handling of any glass object. The mere touch of good glass would put Ronnie in a happy mood.

From the fastness of the stores we unearthed a really lovely old cut glass bottle. It was one that must have been at some time in an old fashioned chemist's shop, for the word "Opoponax" was still faintly visible on the grimy, though once gilt, label. It was filthy, the deep cuts ingrained with the dirt of ages, and the inside so stained that it took me a long time with acids, detergents, and strong alkali rinses before I could get it clear. Once it was cleaned and polished it proved to be a real old beauty, and Ronnie was delighted at the prospect of carrying and presenting it. We were all pretty vague as to what frankincense looked like, but once more the pharmacy came to the rescue.

After a lot of grubbing about in the cellar among the dust and cobwebs, Mr. Thorpe produced a long forgotten rusty tin of some ancient and absolute resin. Throughout the years it had welded into a solid block at the bottom of the tin, but Ted was called on the job and spent a long and noisy afternoon, sitting on the cellar stairs, hacking it out with a chisel. The broken lumps in the cut glass bottle looked extremely effective and, set on a tray draped with a piece of black velvet it made a very elegant and imposing gift.

For the part of Balthazar, who by tradition was a dark-skinned man, we roped in a Jamaican patient, Charlie. He was a magnificent creature standing a good six foot four, and beautifully proportioned. Poor Charlie was just plain simple; good hearted, sweet tempered, but completely incapable of doing the slightest thing without instruction. Catherine and I, both on the small side, would get hold of the huge Charlie and push and shove him about between us, while we tried to drill him into the simple actions of his part. He would beam down at us with his wide brilliant smile, much as an elephant might look down at a couple of Shetland ponies in a circus. But he was a gentle, amiable soul, and once he had got hold of what we wanted him to do, he never gave us a moment's trouble.

The gift of myrrh was a first prize headache. Myrrh in its natural form is an unimpressive-looking sort of resinous substance, and how to make a good showy gift out of that, cost us a lot of thought. There is a pharmaceutical tincture of myrrh, and someone made the bright suggestion that the bottle from the pharmacy might do; but as one seldom keeps more than an ounce or so as it is very seldom used, we decided that a minute bottle would hardly suit the case. Also, as someone else pointed out brightly, it was more than unlikely that Balthazar had presented the Christ Child with a small bottle of tincture of myrrh.

We compromised on the Myrrh. It was altogether too tricky. Eleanor and the other doctors were not able to help with our preparations and rehearsals, as they were on duty at all odd hours, but they took a great interest in our activities. Catherine and I had come to a dead end over this myrrh business, and at one of our evening gatherings we threw the problem open to discussion and begged for suggestions. The gifts of gold and frankincense had been handed round and much admired, then Gillian got the winning idea.

"I've got a biscuit tin shaped like a sort of casket," she said. "If I can find it, what about fixing it on a silver tray and painting it to look like cedar wood, set with gems? It is just as likely that Balthazar presented the myrrh in a casket as anyhow else."

This met with great applause. Gillian dashed off and presently returned with the tin, which proved to be half full of forgotten toffees. We spent the rest of the evening chewing the toffees and congratulating Gillian on her remarkable brain power. We all agreed that she was thrown away as a psychiatrist.

Some of the extra parts which Catherine had introduced specially for the younger patients, were those of Pages in attendance of the Three Kings. The one selected as Caspar's page was an exceedingly pretty girl of about seventeen. She had lovely smooth brown hair of a perfect page-boy length, huge blue eyes, and a gorgeous complexion. Her great failing was her habit of "gawping". If anything caught her attention Maureen would stop stock still, whatever she was doing, her mouth open, while she stated and stared. It was a common cry round the hospital,

"Maureen, stop gawping!"

When she remembered to keep her mouth shut, she looked almost completely normal, but at any moment that awful, open-mouthed stare would appear, and up would go the cry, "Maureen, shut your mouth, and don't gawp!"

It was one thing to teach the individual patients their parts, and we rehearsed them till they appeared quite perfect. Then came the awful moment of rehearsing two or more of them together. Old Arthur, as

Caspar, and Maureen as his page, very nearly drove Catherine and me, as we agreed, "down to Fives."

The actions were very simple. Arthur was to stride on to the stage, bow low before the Crib, then clap his hands high in the air with a flourish. Maureen was to follow carrying the gift and kneel a yard or two behind him while he made his obeisance. When Arthur clapped his hands, she was to rise, move round in front of him, drop on one knee, and hand him the gift, which he then presented at the Crib.

Simple enough - but could we get them to do it?

Arthur was a tall, fine looking old man with a grey beard. If by dint of constant prodding we could make him remember to stand up straight and not shuffle his feet, he made a dignified and imposing figure.

"Stand up straight, Arthur," Catherine adjured him, "clap your hands smartly right up in front of your face. Remember, you are a great King, an Eastern Potentate, and don't look round to see if Maureen is there. Kings don't look round for their pages, they expect them to be there when they clap for them."

Taking a firm grip of the old man, she marched him on to the stage and halted him in front of the broken old chair which was doing duty for the Crib. Meantime I was piloting Maureen in their wake.

Maureen learned her part very much more quickly than Arthur did. Coaching Arthur nearly reduced Catherine and me to nervous wrecks, but eventually he got it, and once Arthur had learned his part he had got it for keeps. He could be seen practising all over the place in the corridors, in the grounds, and up and down the path through the woods. He would suddenly straighten up, take several strides forward, manipulating imaginary robes with great aplomb, make a deep obeisance to the radiator or a tree stump, or anything to hand, then clasp his hands high up before his face in the most lordly manner. Any stranger seeing this performance would have thought the poor old chap even more scatty than he really was.

The Christmas show this year was planned on far more ambitious lines than had ever been attempted before. For one thing, all the previous shows had been tableaux pure and simple with no actions introduced. The hospital orchestra and choir made up of staff and patients, and under the conductorship of one of the Charge Nurses had led the singing of carols while the tableaux were being shown.

Since the previous Christmas, however, a patient had been admitted who was a most remarkable pianist. He had had a world-wide reputation, and it was a terrible tragedy and loss to the world of music when his brain and nerves had broken down under the strain of constant public performances. Godfrey was allowed to have his own magnificent piano in a small room adjoining his ward, and hour after hour, day in and day out, that block rang and resounded with the most glorious music. As long as he was left undisturbed at the keyboard, Godfrey was, to all appearances, perfectly normal. Away from it, he was one of the most difficult and disturbed patients in the hospital. He was kept under the heaviest sedation I had ever seen. This had the effect of reducing the disturbance of the affected part of his brain, while releasing that part which lived in the world of music and allowing it to develop and flourish. Some of the staff had heard him play on the concert platform before his breakdown, and they told me that, brilliant as he was then, he was now, though a pathetic and almost sub-human wreck, even more brilliant and glorious than before.

Godfrey was sometimes allowed to perform at the hospital concerts, but always had to play from behind a light curtain or screen, or else in some position from which he was unable to see the audience. The mere sight of an audience, and still more, the knowledge that the audience could see him, tipped him over the edge at once. Also, there was always a male nurse in plain clothes in attendance.

It was chiefly due to the acquisition of Godfrey that changes had been planned in the Christmas Show. It was felt that a pianist of his calibre should be given as worthy a backing as possible. He was remarkably sane and amenable when discussing the programme, and undertook to play excerpts from the Classics and the Oratorios while the scenes were being acted. The orchestra and choir were to lead in the singing of the carols while the scenes were being changed. Godfrey was well aware that there would be an audience, but as long as he was not under the battery of all those eyes, he was quite content.

At last came the day of the Dress Rehearsal. The audience was composed of those patients whose condition made in inadvisable for them to be present at the real performance. It was unspeakably touching to watch those rows of poor, vacant faces, gradually lighting up under the old-age charm and beauty of the Christmas Story.

At the Dress Rehearsal Catherine as producer, and I as unofficial assistant producer, worked hectically behind the scenes to get our performers into their costumes and make-up. We watched anxiously from the wings as scene after scene went through without a hitch. I was jubilant, but Catherine, who was more experienced than I in theatrical affairs, was not so happy.

"A good Dress Rehearsal is unlucky," she said. "If the Dress Rehearsal is a flop it always means that the real performance will be a success, and vice versa. You mark my words, we are going to hit a snag on the night.

On the night, the hall was packed. The front rows were reserved from the M.S., his wife and party of friends, the Heads of Departments and their friends, the Hospital Committee and Officers, Matron, and her inevitable shadow, then the Sisters and Charge Nurses. Further back were the close packed ranks of patients. Many of the V.I.P.s had turned up in evening dress, and the M.S. resplendent in boiled shirt and white tie, was seated exactly in the centre of the front row. There was a far larger attendance than usual, for it had become known that Godfrey, whom many of them had heard in concerts and on radio before his breakdown, was to play. His own piano had been brought down and set in a position whence, behind his screen, he could see all that went on, on the stage. It was left entirely to him to play whatever he thought suitable, and he did it magnificently.

The first scene - the Annunciation - was quite enchanting. Doris, a gentle, sweet-faced girl from Sevens, in the part of the Madonna, and Peter, a tall graceful lad from Twos, in the part of the Angel Gabriel, played their parts to perfection. From the first moment Catherine and I, in the wings, caught the unmistakable atmosphere which tells that the performance holds the full attention and sympathy of the audience.

The next scene - the Shepherds - went equally well, though we had to keep a wary eye on the Third Shepherd. He was an inveterate smoker and spent most of his time wandering round the hospital and grounds picking up cigarette ends, as he had always spent all his weekly pocket money on cigarettes by Wednesday. Picking up cigarette ends was such a habit with him, that we were terrified lest he should start searching for them all over the stage. St. Joseph managed to keep his eyes demurely on the Crib instead of ogling the Leading Angel as we had feared. We had given both St. Joseph and the Leading Angel a terrific lecture before letting them go on stage, threatening the direst penalties if there was the slightest hint of their usual tickle and slap, however surreptitious. The Leading Angel had coloured blood in her, and was truly a lovely creature, with the dark vivid beauty that so often goes with it. But she was a nymphomaniac, and had the temper of a fiend, and was constantly in trouble for throwing plates or shoes or suchlike at a moment's notice.

Then came the big scene of the Adoration of the Magi. This was to merge into the Grand Finale when all the performers were to come on stage and group themselves round the Crib while the final carol was sung. By now Catherine and I were in such a state of nervous tension and exhaustion, that we were nearly dizzy.

Arthur, in his role of Caspar, was magnificent. Catherine gave his robes a final tweak, set his crown straight and gave him a gentle push. He strode on with a flourish, while I patted Maureen's last hair into place, and hissed in her ear, "Now, remember what you are doing, keep your eyes on Arthur, and don't gawp".

She glided in gracefully after him, dropped on one knee, holding the golden gift exactly as we had taught her. Arthur made a sweeping obeisance to the Crib, then stood up straight and regal, and clapped his hands smartly, high before his face.

Nothing happened.

Catherine, watching from the wings, put out a frantic hand and clutched me.

"Oh, no," she wailed in an agonised whisper, "it isn't true. Maureen has gone off in a gawp!"

"No"! I gasped, "she can't have. What's she gawping at?"

"Come here where I am and have a look."

Clasping each other in an agony, we moved so that we could see what had caught Maureen's wandering eye.

There, right in the centre of the front row, was the M.S., and, by some unlucky trick, one of the lights was reflecting brilliantly from his high, bald head, so that it looked exactly as if he were wearing a halo. Maureen, kneeling close behind Arthur, was staring at this, her mouth wide open, with the golden gift dropping from her hand, completely oblivious of all else.

Arthur kept his head in the most exemplary manner. Raising his hands, he clapped them again.

"Maureen! Maureen," we whispered frantically, "Maureen! Don't gawp!"

But it was no good. Maureen was away well and truly, and short of going on stage and shaking her, there was nothing we could do.

Once again Arthur clapped his hands. Again, no response.

Arthur's patience snapped.

Taking a grip on his crown, he swung round, gave Maureen a good jab with his thumb, and, in stentorian tones which echoed throughout the length and breadth of the hall he roared,

"Oy! Wake up, you little b….!"

CHAPTER 10

My last and finest blow-up was with the Matron. I want to emphasise the point that I am not in the habit of going about looking for trouble, nor would I, in the ordinary way, ever dream of having rows with the Senior Admin. Staff. I know my place in the hospital hierarchy and keep to it. But if people tread on my tail, I am apt to explode. My tail is a delicate and fragile flower, and if trodden on too hard and too frequently I take off vertically, without warning, and come down fighting. We all suffered from this sense of being down-trodden and to such an acute extent that Eleanor and I and the rest of our gang, banded ourselves together as "The Worms."

Often when I have dropped on anybody all teeth and claws, I am sorry for them as soon as the dust has settled, but I was genuinely sorry for the Matron, quite apart from the slanging I gave her.

For one thing, she was much too young and inexperienced for the job. She had obtained it by sheer toadying and favouritism, and it was far too big for her. If she had had the decency to admit this, and had treated the Sisters properly, they would have backed her up through thick and thin, and helped her out with the utmost loyalty. Many of them were women in their fifties, who had spent a lifetime in that hospital, and when Matron was first appointed they were, all of them, prepared to rally round her and do their utmost to make her regime a success.

But she was too swollen-headed to accept their help, and too mean-minded to admit that she needed it. She was a State Registered Nurse, which none of the older Sisters were, and she knew as well as they did that on this account, as well as their age and hopes of a pension, they dared not leave, dared not even stand up to her and her bullying. She would humiliate them in every possible way, even before the junior staff and the patients. One of her pet methods was to ring for one or another of them and order her to come to her office. When the Sister knocked on the door, Matron would deliberately keep her waiting fifteen or twenty minutes in the corridor, before admitting her. Patients, ward-maids, porters, everybody passed up and down that corridor, and it was a shameful and pitiful sight to see an elderly, grey-haired Sister wearily waiting there till Matron should deign to let her enter. It was common property all over the hospital. In many ways Matron defeated her own ends by these methods, for everyone had known and respected, and often loved, the Sisters for many years, and their sympathies were entirely with them and against the Matron.

If left to herself Matron would not have been nearly as bad as she was. Her evil genius, Miss Dalton, was more to blame than she. Miss Dalton was a far more educated woman than Matron, far cleverer and a far stronger character. She was always at Matron's side, flattering, toadying, hinting, whispering. She had got Matron completely under her thumb, and her advice was always bad. Behind Matron's back she would countermand her orders and make her appear incompetent and ridiculous in the eyes of the M.S. and the Committee, while cunningly preserving the facade of assiduous support and help. Everyone knew that she was playing to get Matron deposed, so that she could secure the position for herself, but Matron was too weak, and too blinded by Miss Dalton's wiles to be aware of this. It was she who put Matron up to the trick of keeping people waiting in the corridor. She tried it on me once.

I had occasion to go to Matron's office about something, which was not particularly pressing. I knew they were both in the office as I had seen them go in only a few minutes before, but I had to knock three times before the door was opened by Miss Dalton. Without giving me a chance to speak, she snapped,

"Matron is busy. You will have to wait."

And shut the door in my face. But not before I had caught sight of Matron lolling in an armchair with a cigarette and newspaper.

I was not having any of this waiting business, so I marched back to the pharmacy and got on with my job.

Presently along came Miss Dalton in a towering rage at being foiled of the satisfaction of playing her usual game of humiliating somebody.

"Why didn't you wait as I told you to?" she snarled.

"If you want to see Matron you must come at once."

I took not the slightest notice. Very carefully and deliberately I finished the job on hand, then said in a casual and off-hand manner, "I can't come now. I'm busy. I will come when I find it convenient."

I did not even bother to look round, but I could feel her eyes boring savagely into the back of my neck. She went off, slamming the pharmacy door viciously. As soon as she had gone I turned around to see the gentle Mr. Thorpe gazing at me.

"What was all that about?" he asked mildly.

"Just paying them back a bit of their own coin," I grinned. "They tried that waiting game on me, and I spiked their guns. Do them good for a change."

The explosion was the outcome of several factors, each one indicative of Matron's slackness and Miss Dalton's neglect of her duty. The latter was responsible for the running of the Nurses' Home, but, as I had learned from Daphne, she never went over there, or took the least notice of what went on there. Naturally the maids neglected their work, and the younger nurses, men and girls, got completely out of hand.

It was early in the New Year that I began to notice that my room, which was never cleaned out properly, but did at least get a mop and duster flicked round occasionally, had not been touched for days. Daphne had left some time previously, and matters had deteriorated badly since her departure. The dust lay thick on the dressing table, and rolls of fluff were forming under the bed and round the legs of the furniture. I mentioned this to the Sister who had the room next door. She was one of the elderly ones, who had been there a long time, and although we did not see much of each other, as she was on night duty, we were on very good terms.

"It is always like that now," she said sadly, “the maids have no supervision, and of course they never do a stroke more work than they can help. I have bought all my own cleaning things and I do my own room. I even do my own fire and carry up the coal myself. Otherwise nothing would get done at all.

"But that's all wrong," I cried indignantly, "you shouldn't be expected to do that sort of thing. Is it true that Miss Dalton is supposed to be responsible for the Nurses' Home?"

She looked very uncomfortable, but nodded agreement.

"We daren't say a word," she said, almost in a whisper, "Matron wouldn't hear a thing against her, and in any case, no one can ever get an interview with Matron without Miss Dalton being there. We just haven't a chance, any of us."

I was seething with anger at the utter injustice of it all, but Sister was such a sweet soul that I forced myself to speak lightly.

"Leave this to me" I said, "I am going to have a word with Matron, and if Miss Dalton puts her nose in, she will get it bitten, that's all."

Sister looked at me with relief in her eyes, but this immediately changed to fear.

"Please," she pleaded, "please don't mention that you have spoken to me. Keep my name out of it, won't you? If Miss Dalton knows I have spoken about her she will have her knife into me worse than ever."

"Don't worry, my dear," I replied reassuringly, "I give you my word that I shall not mention a thing about you. I shan't even say that I have spoken to any of the Sisters at all. I know how she treats you, and it makes me livid."

After this, I put little bits of paper and scraps in strategic positions about my room, waiting for my opportunity.

Meantime I chalked up something else to be mentioned to Matron.

The only toilet I had been able to find near the pharmacy was one which was used by the ward maids and patients also by all the patients' friends on visiting days. It was not until later that I learned that there was another, quite nearby, which was used by Matron and the Sisters, and which was kept locked. I should, of course, have been shown this one and given a key, as in my capacity of pharmacist, I rank with the Sisters. In all properly administered hospitals I sit at the Sisters' table and use their sitting room, and my bedroom is always in the Sisters' wing.

It was a Wednesday afternoon, visiting day, and I found a huge queue of patients and their friends in the toilet, out on the corridor, and down the stairs. Children were clamouring and screaming, and the general appearance of the visitors, let alone the patients, made me shudder to think of the state that the toilet would be in. After visiting hours were over, I went to have a look, and my worst fears were realised. The place was appalling. Children, and apparently adults also, had found the floor more convenient than the proper receptacle. Paper, banana skins, toffee wrappers, cigarette ends and everything imaginable were on that floor, and the pan and seat were unspeakable.

Thursday came. The place had not been touched. Friday came, Saturday came, still no one had made any attempt to clean it up. The patients and maids did not seem to mind, and they continued to use it quite happily. By this time, I had found another, at the far end of the main corridor but it was a waste of precious minutes to have to run right down there, and I was beginning to boil up both over this, and over my bedroom, which still had not been touched.

I went home at the weekend, and on Monday morning felt pretty sure that both my room and the toilet would have been cleaned. However, I found that both were exactly as they had been when I left. It was twelve days since I had put the scraps of paper about my room as a check, and I had marked off the days on my calendar. It was certainly longer than twelve days since it had been done, as I had not checked it up at once, but this was enough to go on. I was quite furious enough about that on that Monday morning, but when I found the toilet still untouched, I was just ready for an explosion. As luck would have it, I saw Matron in the corridor, her head in a cupboard, apparently counting blankets. I did not think that counting blankets was part of a Matron's job, but I may be mistaken. The main thing was that she was alone, Miss Dalton nowhere in sight. Not that I should have worried if she had been, I was far too angry to care.

I walked up to her. "Good morning, Matron," I said icily, "I would like to have a word with you."

She returned my greeting civilly enough, but there must have been something in my face or voice, for a look of alarm came into her eyes.

"I wish to report to you that that lavatory is in a perfectly disgraceful condition. It has not been cleaned since last Wednesday, and it is becoming completely insanitary."

There was no mistaking the fear in her face now, as she replied hastily, "That is nothing to do with me. You should tell the cleaners about it."

"I have nothing to do with the cleaning staff," I replied, and was surprised at the cold, suppressed rage in my own voice. "You are the Matron, and I am reporting it to you. I hold you ultimately responsible."

There was a rush of feet as Miss Dalton tore down the corridor and thrust herself between us.

"What's all this about?" she began, but I cut her short.

"Be quiet," I said, "and don't interfere. This is nothing to do with you, and you should know better than to interrupt when I am addressing myself to the Matron."

They both stared at me, and I saw the Matron turn white. They both came of the breed that is accustomed to voices being raised in anger and would have been able to cope with an exhibition of that sort. But a quiet, controlled anger was entirely foreign to them, and scared the daylights out of them.

"There is something else I wish to report," I went on, my voice as baleful as a basilisk, "my bedroom over at the Nurses' Home has not been cleaned for at least twelve days. It is certainly longer than that, but I know it is twelve days because I have checked it off on my calendar. It is in a perfectly disgraceful state. I am not asking who is responsible for the Nurses' Home," I continued, and heard a gasp of rage from Miss Dalton, "but whoever it is, is being guilty of gross neglect of duty."

Suddenly my self-control snapped.

"Go and see for yourselves," I stormed, "go and look at that lavatory, and see if you think it is a credit to the hospital. Go and look at my room and see if you would like yours to be in the same state. Come out of that blanket cupboard and stop staring like a couple of hypnotised rabbits. Call yourselves Matron and Assistant Matron! I have never come across such a place as this in my life, and I hope I never do again!"

I flung away and marched back to the pharmacy. The air all round me must have been sparkling and crackling, for Mr. Thorpe looked at me somewhat apprehensively.

"Anything the matter?" he asked quietly.

"I have just been telling Matron and Miss Dalton a few home truths," I replied. "I don't think they liked it very much, but it has made me feel a lot better."

Being a wise man, he merely raised his eyebrows and said nothing. As usual, after I have blown my top, I suddenly saw the funny side of it, and began to laugh, and told him all about it.

"You told them they were a couple of hypnotised rabbits?" he exclaimed, in tones of utter incredulity.

"Well, so they were," I replied scornfully, "they are just a couple of swollen headed bullies, and if anyone stands up to them they collapse at once."

Actually, I found it in my heart to pity Matron, though I had no pity for Miss Dalton. Matron, deprived of her support had shown herself in true colours. She was a weak, mean character, wholly without any natural poise or dignity. She was in a position which was far too big for her and was merely a tool in Miss Dalton's hands. In a lesser position, and under a good influence, she would have been very different, but under the strain of trying to keep up her dignity, striving to present to the M.S. and the Committee that she knew her job and was doing it well, conscious of her own incompetence, utterly unsure of herself, and relying entirely upon Miss Dalton to uphold her, she was well on the way to becoming a nervous wreck.

Towards the end of the morning I went along to the lavatory again. To my intense amusement it was completely spotless, polished and immaculate. The floor shone as it had never shone before, the seat was freshly scrubbed, the pan cleaner than I had ever seen it, the wash-basin virginal, and even the taps and door handle had been polished.

To give Matron her due, she was a fast worker once an idea had been put into her head, even if it needed putting in with a sledge hammer. Somebody had been put through the hoop, and I grinned in unholy glee at the thought.

That evening when I went back to the Nurses' Home, the same transformation scene had been enacted in my bedroom. The place had been spring-cleaned from top to toe, and smelt sweet and fresh, and redolent of floor and furniture polish.

While I was standing admiring it, one of the maids came hurrying in. She was a very nice woman, older and more conscientious than the rest of the young daily girls, but she only came in one or two days a week. She was nearly in tears.

"Oh, what have you been saying to Matron?" she exclaimed. "She and Miss Dalton came rushing over here like a couple of mad things this morning, and they fair tore the place to pieces. Went around all the rooms and scolded and carried on at us, you never heard the like. They had all the girls crying and fair scared silly. You never saw such carryings on. Said you had complained your room hadn't been cleaned for a fortnight."
"Well, it hadn't," I replied, "it was in a disgraceful state. You must have seen it for yourself."

"But couldn't you have spoken to me or Edith or one of the girls?" she wailed, "not go straight to Matron like that. It was terrible. I've been coming here six years now, and Matron has never been over here more than once or twice to my certain knowledge, and then she comes over raging and creating fit to raise the dead. And that Miss Dalton, what's supposed to be in charge here, tagging on round after her and telling us off worse than Matron herself. Oh, why didn't you speak to one of us?"

"I couldn't do that," I replied, "it is not my business to give orders to the household staff. If I have a complaint to make I go directly to the person responsible. I give orders in my own department, but not in other people's. I am sorry if you got into trouble, for I know you don't work in this wing, but you see my position, don't you?"

Thence forward my room was kept meticulously clean, but the entire house staff regarded me even more warily than did the dining room and finance office staffs.

It was halfway through January, when I had only another fortnight to go, that the cold weather and nerve strain got me down. My old enemy, bronchitis, descended upon me. I fought it as long as I could, but it developed into virus pneumonia, and I was forced to pack up. My husband Doc came over by car, scooped up me and my belongings, and whirled me home.

It had been a strange and quite unique experience at that hospital, and in spite of everything, when the time came I was genuinely sorry to leave. I had made closer and more lasting friendships there than I ever have elsewhere, and one after another my friends came to my room, as Doc was helping me to pack, to say goodbye.

"I don't know what the Worms are going to do without you," wailed Eleanor, "we shall be more downtrodden than ever now our champion is leaving us."

"I am going to miss you terribly," said Catherine, "you have been good for us and good for the whole place. Things have been very different here since you came. We have never had anyone with the guts to speak out as you have done, and as soon as you have gone it will just relapse into what it was before."

Doc stopped the car outside the pharmacy, and Mr. Thorpe came out to say goodbye. There were tears in his eyes, though he spoke as quietly as ever.

"This place won't be the same without you," he said, "you have been like a clean wind blowing away the cobwebs. I won't say you haven't had me worried stiff at times, with your way of pitching into everybody in the top positions, but we have never had anyone like you before, and I doubt if we ever shall again."

In the course of the next year I heard that many changes had taken place. I have kept up a brisk correspondence with my friends, and they have kept me up to date with the news. Miss Dalton completely lost her influence over Matron and left a month or two after I did. Freed from her influence, Matron matured and improved to an amazing extent, her manner towards the Sisters changed entirely, and a Warden was engaged, who took very firm charge of the Nurses' Home. The M.S. was due to retire in any case, and his successor proved to be a far better organiser and administrator than he had been.

Later on, both the secretary and the finance officer either left or retired and were succeeded by younger and more competent men. The place must be very different now, but I am told that to this day my name is still remembered and spoken with bated breath.

CHAPTER 11

There are certain well-worn maxims and tags, which have always given me great delight, and in the following of which I have achieved a lot of entertainment and experience.

Among my favourites are:-

- Cast your bread upon the waters.
- Leap before you look (so much more enterprising than in its correct form)
- Fall in the soup (a frequent pastime of mine)
- Dive in bald-headed.
- Have a bash at it.

And in particular that delightful proverb which hails, I think, from the West Indies -

- "If crab no walk he no see nuffin."

These I find particularly encouraging in my career of full-time locum.

Many a time I have answered an advertisement from some locality which I wished to visit, only to be informed that the post was already filled, usually by someone living nearer the area. At first, I was much disappointed and discouraged when this occurred, but I have since learned by experience that it is well worth replying to any advertisement which happens to appeal. Invariably one's application is filed for reference, and it has often happened that, months later, when I have forgotten all about it, a sudden request has come from some place about which I had given up all hopes. Answering advertisements is a wonderful way of casting bread on the waters, and it invariably comes back after many days.

On going to a new place, one never knows what it is going to be like or what one is going to be let in for. It is now that the next series of maxims comes into play. It is necessary to take the leap without much chance of looking first, one has to dive in and have a bash at it. It is quite on the cards that one may fall in the soup, but there is always the consoling thought that the crab is not sitting in a hole and seeing "nuffin". One certainly sees life, if nothing else, and sometimes the bread on the waters comes back with a wonderful dividend.

This happened in the case of a job I got in the Channel Islands. I had never been to the Islands and had always longed to do so, and one autumn I answered an advertisement for a locum who was required in Guernsey. To my bitter disappointment the post was filled by someone in the Island. I took on various other locum jobs and forgot all about it.

The following spring, I was at home for a short break. Doc and I were sitting at lunch when the phone rang and I answered it. To my unspeakable amazement it was from Guernsey. Could I come at once, if not sooner? The pharmacist had been taken ill and was obliged to go to the Mainland for special treatment. There was an experienced unqualified one who could hold the fort for a short time, but the work was too heavy for one, and in any case a qualified pharmacist was essential.

I could not go at once as I was due to start a week's locum almost immediately, but Guernsey was willing to wait for that week, provided I could go directly I was free. This I was only too pleased to agree to, though it involved a frantic amount of preparation, as the day I was due to fly over was the Saturday before Easter. Everyone who has ever flown to the Channel Islands knows what it means to secure a passage at holiday time, in fact air passages are usually fully booked up months ahead. However, by some incredible stroke of good fortune, the agency was able to secure a cancelled booking for me. It was not till I had considerably more experience of booking to the Channel Islands that I realised how amazingly fortunate I had been.

The intervening week's locum was dreary in the extreme. It was at a small branch hospital in the south suburbs of London, where there were very few in-patients, but enormous numbers of Out-Patients. The building had not been designed as a hospital but was a very large old house which had been adapted for the purpose. The pharmacy was appalling, quite the most miserable, poky little hole I have ever worked in. It was, quite literally, hardly larger than a fair-sized cupboard. The arrangements were a disgrace. A large addition had been built on to one side of the house, to serve as the Out-Patients' hall and consulting rooms. This was on the far side of the building from where the pharmacy was situated. The invariable rule in a properly designed hospital, is that the O-P hall adjoins the pharmacy, with a hatch opening through, so that patients can hand in their cards and receive their medicines direct.

In this case the arrangement was that as soon as a patient was given his card, he pressed a button in the O-P hall. This sounded a buzzer in the pharmacy. The pharmacist then had to drop whatever job was in hand, hurry through long and tortuous passages the full length of the house, dodging past stretchers with patients going to the theatre, laundry baskets being filled or emptied, and deliveries of all sorts being taken in, to the O-P hall. There he took the patient's card and hurried the whole way, past all the intervening obstacles in the passages to the pharmacy. Once there, the prescription had to be made up, then the whole double journey had to be done again in order to deliver the medicine to the patient. As often as not, one had just got back to the pharmacy after delivering the medicine, when the buzzer would go once more, and off you went on the rat-race all over again. It was sheer murder, and I have never met anything to equal that place for reckless expenditure of time, energy and temper. How the permanent pharmacist ever put up with it I cannot imagine, but he was a married man with a young family, and had recently bought a house in the neighbourhood, so it was probably that which kept him anchored.

It was entirely unnecessary too, which infuriated me more than anything. A very small amount of adjustment, could by moving the position of the pharmacy, have cut out all that long wearying and time-wasting running to and fro. But it was the same old story. The pharmacist would not speak up for himself and was willing to continue working under these fantastic conditions, sooner than - as he imagined - "make trouble", or risk losing his job. Either making, or not making, trouble, depends upon the temperament of the pharmacist concerned, but the fact remains that no pharmacist now-a-days need put up with unnecessary discomforts or bad working conditions for fear of losing his job. We are in such acute demand that no employer or governing body would dream of dismissing the pharmacist, except for gross inefficiency, or some really serious offence.

As I have proved for myself, it is only necessary to stand up to employers, whoever they may be, and state one's requirements, under threat of resigning if necessary, and they will immediately toe the line. They are better aware of the fact that we are practically irreplaceable, than a great many pharmacists themselves are.

Added to my miseries was the fact that I was not given accommodation in the Nurses' Home. The authorities simply said they were not prepared to supply accommodation and left it at that. I was expected to find my own. As I did not know the district at all, this seemed cavalier treatment to say the least. The pharmacist himself had to find somewhere for me to stay and had great difficulty in doing so. He found me a room with a family who lived a long bus journey away. They were very kind according to their lights, but never again.

Only once since then have I ever taken a post where I was required to live "as family", and that was under pressure of desperate pleading and persuasion from the pharmacist concerned. On every occasion that I have lived in digs or "as family" I have suffered such acute discomfort that now Doc has put his foot down, and forbidden me ever to do it again. It is very seldom indeed that Doc ever takes a firm line with me, and it is invariably for my own protection against my propensity for falling into the soup, and usually at my own request. When I was doing retail work, I so often fell into the soup, that eventually I begged him to forbid me ever to undertake hospital work unless I could be given accommodation in the Nurses' Home. Hospital accommodation varies enormously, but even at its very worst is far better than living in digs or "as family".

The house in which I stayed was in a raw, new building estate, the roads and gardens still unmade and a mass of piles of bricks, concrete mixers and builders' impedimenta. The house inside was spotless, but only because it was brand new, and even in the short time I was there I began to see only too plainly what it would soon deteriorate into. My room was very small, no chest of drawers or wardrobe, not even hanging space for clothes, and only a small rough kitchen table with one drawer; which meant living almost entirely in my suitcase.

The bathroom was a welter of other people's towels, face-cloths, tooth brushes, toilet jars and bottles, with dirty clothes all over the floor. There are few things which make me shudder more than a grubby and cluttered-up bathroom. My bedroom was icy cold, far too cold to sit or write in during the evenings and sitting downstairs with the family was a penance as much for them as for me.

My only consolation with regard to that job came from the old charlady who cleaned the pharmacy. On my last morning she informed me, quite gratuitously, that the place was a palace since I had been there; she had never known it so clean and tidy in all the years she had worked there. It was a fair treat and she only wished "some people" would keep it like that. You wouldn't know I had ever been in it. As she was a tough, hard-boiled old Cockney battle-axe, I positively smirked with virtue, and felt that my trials had not been unrewarded.

I did not have to work on Good Friday, though I did have to work on Saturday morning, which was going to make an awful stampede to get to the airport for Guernsey that same afternoon. It was not worth going home just for Friday, so I took myself out for the day. I had happened to see a bus pass near my digs bearing the name of the western suburb where we lived in my early youth. I therefore climbed on and secured my favourite front seat. I have known the centre of London and all the main arterial roads leading out of it, intimately for most of my life, but the outer suburban areas have always rather eluded me. This bus followed the most surprising route. We meandered through miles upon unrecognisable miles of grisly suburbia, ranging from the smoke-grimed Victorian to the rawness of new building estates. Occasionally we came to the surface at some place which I knew, such as Kew and Hampton Court, then plunged once more into acres upon acres of suburbs, everywhere grey and soulless and swept by an unspeakable east wind.

Eventually we arrived at the area which I had known as a child, but it was so altered and had deteriorated so horribly that, if I had not remembered the names of the streets, I should never have known it.

I was depressed by suburbia, hungry and frozen, so I made my way back to my well-known and beloved stamping grounds in central London.

At my table in the restaurant was a very well-dressed couple who insisted upon telling me their life story. People seem quite addicted to this, though I should not imagine I look the sort of person to be a repository of confidences. But I have perfected a repertoire of Ohs,

Ahs, and Ums, which produced in varying tones of sympathy and interest, seems to draw confidences like a poultice draws boils. In this way I hear all sorts of entertaining stories, while giving nothing away myself.

In this case the wife had just run away with her husband's best friend. The gilt was just beginning to wear off the gingerbread, for the errant wife was tired and edgy, and the husband's best friend was obviously beginning to wonder if he had not been somewhat hasty in annexing the said lady. They had both been consoling themselves alcoholically, and though they were not strictly speaking, drunk, yet they were in the condition of having drink taken. In his attempts to stimulate the lady's waning interest, the husband's best friend repeatedly addressed me as "pet" and "honey girl", pressed cigarettes upon me, which I refused, begged me to let him buy me a drink, which I also refused, and tried to make a date with me for that evening. The last extravaganza took effect, though not quite that which the husband's best friend had intended. The errant wife suddenly appeared to realise that her escort was more of a Don Juan than she had taken him for.

Throwing me a glance of the deepest malevolence, she stood up and announced, "If you are making a date with that," and she glared at me, "I'm going home to Derek," picked up her gloves and handbag and strode out of the restaurant.

The husband's best friend and I stared dumbly at each other, then both collapsed in gales of laughter.

"She had better go home to her Derek if that's how she feels about it," he remarked, cheerfully. "I always suspected she had a temper, but I didn't think she'd turn as bitchy as that. Now then, what about that date for this evening?"

"No, thank you," I replied firmly, "I've got a perfectly good husband of my own, and I don't want anybody else's husband's best friend, thank you all the same."

He shrugged his shoulders good humouredly, and accepted defeat.

"Anyway," he said, "you must let me buy you a box of chocolates. You got me out of a bit of a hole, and you have been a real good sport. It is a change to find a woman who refuses a date just because she happens to be married. What about it? A box of chocolates and no strings?"

I meditated solemnly for a few minutes. "All right," I said somewhat ungraciously, "but if I let you buy me a box of chocolates, will you give me your word that you won't make any more trouble between Derek and his wife?"

"Fair enough," he agreed, "and you can tell your husband, with my regards, that he is a damn sight luckier bloke than most."

It was a fabulous box of chocolates, and Doc laughed his head off when I told him about it and gave him the message.

When corresponding about the post in Guernsey, the hospital Secretary had made a very strong point of the necessity of my sending my passport in advance, as well as bringing my Certificate. I never go to any post without taking the latter, but, knowing that passports are not required for the Channel Islands, I was somewhat surprised. My passport was all in order, so there was no trouble about that.

The Saturday morning was cold and dreary, but I got through it somehow, and leapt into the taxi with cries of delight. It was 10/10 cloud ceiling, but we soon climbed above into glorious sunshine. I am an experienced air traveller, but never have those banks of white cloud spread like a brilliant Arctic scene below, looked more exquisite and exhilarating than they did that day after the purgatory of suburban London.

No sooner had I alighted at Guernsey airport, than I was greeted by name, by a tall pleasant man, who apparently recognised me from my passport photograph. There were numerous other passengers in the plane, and I am still wondering if it were a compliment or otherwise.

Immediately our greetings were over, he asked me to wait while he phoned some V.I.P. in St. Peter Port. He then put me and my luggage in a taxi and whirled me off to the States Offices in the middle of the town. On the way he asked if I had my Certificate. I said yes, but that it was packed at the bottom of my large case. Then and there, in the taxi, he helped me unpack, extricate the Certificate, and stuff everything back again. It was all very breathless, as I had not had any warning that I should be required to prove my credentials almost before I had got my feet on the ground.

My new friend explained that in Guernsey the law requires that all doctors, pharmacists, dentists and veterinary surgeons must receive Authorisation from H.M. Attorney General before being allowed to practise their profession. Furthermore, they must appear before the States and prove their credentials at the next Sitting of the Court after their arrival.

This was all very exciting. I have never yet had the experience of being required to take an Oath on the Bible and asked eagerly if I should have to do so.

My friend would not say definitely, and I gathered it rather depended upon whether the Court was in a good temper or not.

I asked why I had had to send my passport in advance, in fact why it was necessary to produce it at all.

"For purposes of identification," he replied rather severely.

"But I've got my Certificate," I said.

"Ah, yes," he said, "but the Court has to satisfy themselves that you are the person named on the Certificate."

Dear me, I thought to myself, I might as well be Mata Hari in the flesh, despite all appearances to the contrary. It is a fascinating experience to be regarded with deep suspicion, knowing all that time that one is impeccably innocent, and can prove it. I was thoroughly enjoying myself.

On arrival at the States Offices we were ushered with great ceremony into the presence of H.M. Attorney General. There seemed to be quite a lot of protocol, and I could only hope that I acquitted myself as well as could be expected. The Attorney General was extremely brisk and business-like, but very human and pleasant. The offices were large, light and modern, and there seemed to be clerks and variegated officials all over the place, in spite of its being Saturday afternoon. I learned later that in Guernsey a Saturday is an ordinary full working day. The Island's half day is Thursday. This is on account of the tomatoes, for the economic structure of the Island is built on tomatoes, with the tourists and visitors running second. The shipments of tomatoes have to be got out on Saturday for the weekend market on the Mainland.

H.M. Attorney General examined my passport and my Certificate and produced a copy of the Register of the Pharmaceutical Society and checked me up on that too. They are nothing if not thorough in Guernsey. He then pronounced himself satisfied and issued me with a provisional licence to practise till the next Sitting of the Court, which was to be the following Friday, when I was required to appear.

My friend then drove me to the hospital. It is a perfectly delightful place, standing high up on a hill some little distance from St. Peter Port. The Nurses' Home, new since the Occupation, is quite one of the best I have ever stayed in. Everything was modern, bright and attractive, wash basins and radiators in the bedrooms, divan beds with interior sprung mattresses, plenty of drawer space and a large wardrobe. The Matron was on leave, but the Deputy Matron took me under her wing and looked after me like a mother. After the discomforts and miseries of the preceding locum job, I felt I was in the seventh heaven.

Being early spring the country was at it's most exquisite. Camellia bushes and magnolias were in flower, and rhododendrons were all ready to burst. The primroses and daffodils covered the banks in carpets and drifts, and the glorious, unearthly green of the budding trees took one's breath away. I have been to the same hospital every year since, but never again in the spring time. It is a jewel of an island, and a large piece of my heart is rooted there, but I shall never forget my first sight of it in the freshness of that incredible spring.

Having arrived on the afternoon of the Saturday before Easter, I had two whole days, Easter Sunday and Monday, free, before starting work on the Tuesday. I had had to cross on the Saturday, as that was the only plane reservation available. The weather was superb, and I made the very most of my freedom. On those two days, and the ensuing Thursday afternoons and Sundays, I did all the Island coach trips. I went to Herm, I went to Sark and all my outings and expeditions were given a keener edge of enjoyment by the fact that I had to work, and work hard, at my job all the rest of the time. I enjoyed them far more than I should have done had I been there merely as a holiday maker.

Until the Friday came, when I was to appear before the Court, I had a sensation that I was only there on sufferance or probation, despite my provisional licence, (which I still keep and cherish as one of my greatest treasures) but at last the great day came.

My Mentor told me to be ready at a quarter to ten and to bring my passport and Certificate. I thought I might as well try to look as efficient and competent as possible so put on a neat, tailored grey suit, with spotless white blouse and gloves. My only concession to frivolity was a very dashing little red hat, to which I matched my lipstick very carefully.

He drove me down to the Court House, an imposing granite building in the middle of St. Peter Port. The actual Court Room, which corresponds to our House of Commons, was - I believe - being redecorated. In any case the Court was not sitting there, but in the Police Court below. This was very small to my Mainland eyes, but beautifully appointed, neat and perfect in every detail.

At the back of the room were some half dozen rows of benches, rising on shallow steps, and on one of these we took our seat. Below were two witness boxes, one on either side, with small wrought iron gates between. Beyond lay the main body of the hall, with tables and desks down each side. At the opposite end were two large windows, and between them the Bailiff's Chair, beneath a huge carved Royal Coat of Arms. There were other tables to right and left of the Bailiff's Chair, facing down the hall.

When we arrived, the little gates were open, and there was a scurry of activity going on. There were several groups of people on the benches near us, and the main part of the hall was like an ants' next, with extremely busy gentlemen dashing to and fro with briefcases, all looking too important to be true. As we sat and waited, the Attorney General came to have a word with us, just checking up that I had my necessary documents, and briefing me as to procedure. My Mentor whispered to me that I was the big show that day. All the other cases concerned the Islanders themselves, but it was very seldom that an outsider from the Mainland was to be admitted publicly and officially to the community. I fairly wriggled with excitement.

Then a constable appeared and called to us to be silent and stand as the Bailiff entered and took his seat. Then the Bailiff, the late Sir Ambrose Sherwill, was a tall, handsome, and most distinguished-looking man. He, as Bailiff was Head of the States, a position similar to our Prime Minister. The name of Sir Ambrose Sherwill is engraved on the hearts of the Islanders for his magnificent leadership during the horrors of the Occupation and will go down to history as one of the greatest of Guernsey's sons.

The proceedings opened with several cases of transfer of property. All sales of property in the Island have to be approved by the Bailiff and Court. There was an atmosphere of cosy friendliness about it all. Little groups of people were gathered about the tables and desks, each party represented by their own solicitor. Occasionally two opposing solicitors would work up a brisk and acrimonious argument, but one had the feeling the whole time that it was just part of the show and thrown in for good measure. Off duty they were probably the best of friends, had known each other all their lives, and had punched each other's heads in the schoolroom. The Bailiff looked on in a benevolent and paternal fashion, occasionally putting in a quiet word or query, as he leaned back comfortably in the great chair. It was a family party pure and simple, though conducted throughout with the most punctilious ceremony.

When these cases were finished, my name was called. Immediately the atmosphere changed, and everyone, even the Bailiff, sat up straight in their chairs. Gone was the relaxed friendliness of the family conclave, and instead I was acutely aware of the surge of suspicion, almost of active hostility, sweeping over the hall. I was an outsider, I was an unknown, and the age-old instinct of the clan, which, however much they may fight among themselves, unite at once to present a strong face to any stranger, took command. It was neither conscious nor intentional, but it was there unmistakeably. The atmosphere was crystallised by the action of the constable. All this time the little gates had been open, with everyone passing freely to and fro. Now he came forward and shut them with a clang. I, the outsider, the unknown, had to take my place at the locked gates and stand alone, for inspection and recognition. It was a most curious and dramatic experience.

In dead silence I left my seat and moved to my place at the little gates. Fortunately, I have never suffered from any form of self-consciousness or stage fright, and I was too keenly interested in everything to think of anything else. There is also something to be said for having been in the Army. If nothing else, it does at least teach you to stand stock still under a battery of critical eyes. I came smartly to attention, and just allowed my eyes to glance round at those keen, hard Island faces, while I felt the shrewd eyes boring into me from all sides. It seemed to be definitely a ceremony of recognition, for I stood there, motionless in the middle of the silent Court for several minutes.

Then the Attorney General stood up and addressed the Bailiff. He made a long speech about me, giving all particulars. How he had seen me immediately on my arrival in the Island, how he had checked my passport and Certificate and granted me a provisional licence. He then produced the Pharmaceutical Register and opened it at my name and read out the paragraph relating to myself. The Bailiff asked me if all these facts were correct, and I said they were. The Register, together with my passport and Certificate, were then handed to the Bailiff for inspection. He studied them and passed them on to the stern-faced men seated to right and left of him. They were all the highest dignitaries of the Island, with wonderful old titles dating from Norman times. I am not attempting to name them, much as I wish I could.

They all sat round drinking me in with the utmost solemnity while this was going on. When the Bailiff and the others had inspected my credentials, the Bailiff expressed himself satisfied that I should be granted a full licence and called for a show of hands. There was no dissentient voice. He turned to me with a smile and thanked me and said that everything was perfectly in order. I smiled, bowed, and returned to my seat.

The moment Sir Ambrose expressed himself satisfied, the atmosphere changed again. The stern, hard faces relaxed, the keen eyes no longer raked me mercilessly from head to foot, but there were smiles and nods all round. The atmosphere was warm and friendly once more, but now I was included in it. I was one of the clan, a member of that wonderful Island community, I was accepted as a working member of the team. I was no longer a stranger, no longer even a visitor to be merely tolerated for the money I spent, but a true and accepted member of that proud, independent and heroic island.

Never again should I have to stand for recognition. Each time I have been to work there subsequently, I have taken over the job without the slightest query being raised. I have been accepted by the Law of the Island, and no further recognition or licence is necessary. It is one of the proudest and most exhilarating memories of my life.

My only slight disappointment was that I had not been required to take an Oath on the Bible. My Mentor told me that my credentials had been in such perfect order that this was not considered necessary. But this had not been the case with a locum they had had from the Mainland some time previously.

Apparently, he had never had a passport, and had not considered it necessary to obey instructions when informed that it was essential to produce one. My Mentor wagged his head sadly as he told me about it.

"The Court kept us here a good two hours," he said, "they just tore him to pieces. They fairly made a meal of him," he went on with a sort of gloomy relish, as if, against his better nature, he also had enjoyed that meal. "I thought they were never going to let us go. They just couldn't or wouldn't agree as to whether he was the person named on the Certificate. The poor chap was worn out, and so was I, by the time they had finished with us".

"They seemed rather to enjoy the chance of a dog-fight," I remarked.

"They do," he agreed, then added sotto voce, "but they can't be compared with the Council of Sark."

From which I gathered that that placid and lovely little island settles its internecine troubles with about as much peace and amity as a cage of wolves over a bone. It would seem that the Dame usually has to wade in and restore order with all the forcefulness and authority for which that splendid lady is so justly famous and beloved.

CHAPTER 13

It was in 1957 that I first went to work in the hospital which was to become my second home for the next nine years. It was a Mental hospital, an enormous place, at that time the second largest in England, with upwards of three thousand patients and there were only two pharmacists to cope with all the dispensing. The work was phenomenal and made all the worse by the fact that the pharmacy was still administered in the style of the mid-twenties. It was a beautiful pharmacy, very spacious and with acres of lovely shelves and cupboards, but the Chief Pharmacist had been there since 1927, and had neither the idea, nor the intention, of modernising in any way whatever. The shelves were beautifully set out with scores of lovely old bottles, many of them of the green fluted glass which are now collectors' pieces, and a row of huge Victorian ointment jars. They all contained ancient preparations which had been out of date for the past forty years. The names of the contents of all the bottles and jars were exquisitely embossed in gold leaf on each container on moulded panels, and the majority of them I had never seen or heard of since my apprenticeship days far back in the early twenties. The bottles and jars stood on the shelves, the regulation few inches apart, taking up an immense amount of space, and hardly one of them was ever used. All the multitudinous new drugs, antibiotics, tranquillisers and the like, which were in constant use, were pushed away in corners, or under the benches or stairs, without the slightest attempt at classification. The amount of extra work that this entailed is quite unimaginable.

Any suggestion of mine that a bit of re-arrangement would help to ease the work and speed it up, was met by a shocked and stony refusal, as if I had suggested something sacrilegious.

The hospital stood in huge grounds with extensive playing fields and a large and flourishing farm on which many of the patients were employed. Towards the end of my years there the farm was given up, as the patients' condition had improved so immensely with the use of the new drugs, that they could be employed on simple commercial enterprises, whereby they could earn more money for themselves, besides which the work went a long way towards their rehabilitation and subsequent discharge from hospital. The gardens round the buildings were most beautifully laid out with some of the most glorious flower beds I have ever seen.

The Nurses' Home was modern and comfortable, and over the years successive Wardens passed on from one to the other the information as to which room I preferred, and if it were in any way possible, it was always kept for me. The food was first class, varied, well prepared, well served and lavishly plentiful. Everybody had the same, patients and all. Here there was the system by which every member of the Staff, from the Medical Superintendent downwards, took their midday dinner in the great dining room, all together. Before now I have remarked how this system always seems to propagate a good atmosphere throughout the entire Staff, and it certainly was the case here. Every department was grossly understaffed and overworked, but everybody was friendly and cheerful, the patients were happy and kindly treated, and there was a general air of slap-happy camaraderie which was quite delightful. Of course, we were always tired and all groused like mad, but there was never any ill-feeling behind it, and everyone seemed to adopt the attitude that anything might happen at any moment and usually did.

There was a dance for the patients once a week, and members of the Staff were always welcome to join in; there were two very good cinema shows a week, and some entertainment or other was held almost every evening in the big Hall. Everything was on a colossal scale. I have been told how many miles of corridors there were in the building but have forgotten the figure and am not going to make a guess for fear of being accused of exaggeration. There were forty wards, and during my first years of visiting there, they were all fully occupied, in fact many were overcrowded. As time went on, however, I began to find on each succeeding visit, that more and more wards were being closed, and the numbers of patients decreased the whole time. This was due to the increasing numbers that could be discharged, rehabilitated, and basically this was entirely due to the use of the modern tranquillisers and other drugs.

In spite of the decrease in numbers, the work in the pharmacy increased all the time. This may seem a paradox but was due to the ever-increasing number of new drugs, which were produced in a perfect spate over those years. The Medical Staff were very progressive in their outlook, and constantly trying out the drugs as they came on the market, and it took us all our time to keep up with them.

Sometimes I was there in the capacity of Assistant, then when the Chief was on leave, I took over his job and became Chief. The first time I was there the Senior was on leave, and I was working with the Chief. Unfortunately, the Chief and the Senior were everlastingly at loggerheads, and although they had already been working together for more than ten years, neither could abide the other. Of course, I was never there with both of them at once, and during my first term of duty the Chief warned me that the Senior was lazy and unreliable, and told me that he could not be trusted as Chief, but that I should be taking over the post. This was completely against all protocol. In the absence of the Chief his place is automatically taken on by the Senior, and no locum should ever be brought in over his head. I was distinctly unhappy at the prospect, not that I was afraid of the work as Chief, but very naturally I anticipated all sorts of trouble with the Senior. The Chief told me that the Senior must never touch the Dangerous Drugs or put up the tablets for the patients to take out on week-end leave. As the Senior was qualified in exactly the same way that the Chief and I were, it made me think pretty hard. However, I decided to wait and see, and form my own judgement on the Senior when we met.

As it turned out, I had no trouble at all. The Senior, Mr. Barron, was a huge man, well over six feet in height and big in proportion. He was the most kind-hearted, easy-going soul one could wish to meet. He made no trouble whatever about me, a locum, being promoted over his head; in fact he expressed his delight that it was I who had the responsibility and not he. As we got to know each other his personality expanded like a flower, and he showed himself as a most humorous and likeable companion. The Chief seemed to have a repressive and annihilating effect on him, and not being allowed any responsibility crushed his self-confidence and initiative and made him seem incompetent and lazy. I handed over all normal responsibilities to him, and he rose to every emergency and obviously enjoyed doing so. He proved to be a non-stop worker, also a non-stop talker; the latter propensity drove me distracted at times, and I had no compunction in shutting him up, which he took with the utmost good humour. We became extremely good friends, and I enjoyed working with him far more than with the Chief.

The pharmacy porter was a great character. He was short and stocky, invariably cheerful and efficient, and quite the best of his delightful breed that I have ever met. He and I became very real friends, and I owed more to him in coping with the work than I can ever say. He was approaching retirement age towards the end of my years of locum work there, and after he left the pharmacy was never the same again. He had been on the hospital staff in various capacities for somewhere about forty years, and everyone, staff and patients alike, knew and loved him. I was constantly getting piteous phone calls from various departments and wards - Could you lend us George for a few minutes, our oxygen cylinder - or window latch - or linen cupboard door - has stuck, or Nellie has dropped her hearing aid down behind the radiator, and please let George come and sort it out. He would go bustling off efficient and helpful as ever, invariably returning with a broad grin, and some absurd yarn about his activities. One of his favourite observations on the inefficiency and helplessness of the rest of the Staff was, "'smarvellous, ennit?" When he and Barron and I were in the pharmacy together they were the happiest and most carefree times of my life, despite the back-breaking work and responsibility.

On the first morning of my arrival there I took the opportunity, during the ten minutes coffee break, to go down the long corridor to the hospital shop, to get some biscuits and cigarettes. The pharmacy doors of course, were always kept locked, but the moment I appeared in the corridor I was accosted by a tiny wizened little woman, who firmly barred my way, and unceremoniously demanded, "Oo are you?" I replied politely, that I was the new pharmacist and had just come to work there. She let me pass, but when I returned I found her standing with her back against the pharmacy door holding the side jambs in either hand, completely blocking my entry. I politely asked her to move so that I could get back to my work, but not a bit of it. Thrusting her wrinkled face close to mine she asked in sepulchral tones, "What 'ave you done with the body?" I was completely taken aback, and could think of no better reply than, "Well, I really wouldn't know." She came closer still and said in tones of even deeper suspicion, "Oh, yes, you do, and", with a look of infinite cunning, "what's more, I know too!"

I was so utterly shattered that I had not a word to say, and putting her gently aside, I dodged into the pharmacy and locked the door behind me with a gasp of relief. When I reported my encounter, I was greeted with hoots of laughter.

"Oh, so you've met the old Judge have you?" said George. "I saw her in the corridor and I knew she'd be after you. She always spots every new comer in the place."

I asked why she was called the Judge. They told me that she was believed to have worked as a cleaner at the Old Bailey for many years, and that she knew the details of every criminal case that had been tried there during all that time. She could recite the names of the prisoners, the Judges, the Counsels and everybody connected with all the cases; her mind was constantly running on murders, and the report of a body found in a suitcase in a Left Luggage Office, kept her happy for weeks. George told me that she was quite harmless as long as you let her address you first. If you spoke to her and she did not happen to be in the mood, she would catch you a swipe across the face. He said that she had once sent him flying, small as she was, and stocky as he was. She had a tremendous Cockney sense of humour, and apart from her obsession with murders and corpses was as bright and intelligent as they come.

Barron was extremely kind to the old Judge. Regularly every day she called at the hatch for a gossip and bit of back-chat with him, and he invariably had a little packet of sweets for her. The huge man would lean through the hatch and laugh and tease with the tiny little woman in the corridor, and their conversations were extremely amusing and completely inconsequential. Occasionally snippets reached me, and I remember one tit-bit.

"Go on with you," said Barron, "don't you remember the time you dived into the Thames off the top of the Houses of Parliament?"

"Yus," came the prompt reply, "wi' me long golden 'air a-streamin' in the wind."

Many of the patients were really sweet. There was one old lady who regularly, two or three times a week, popped little packets of chocolate or Smarties through the letter box in the pharmacy door. She always knew how many of us were working there and counted out her little gifts accurately. I never saw her, as she always slipped away without waiting for thanks. One gets so little in the way of any sort of recognition in the course of our work as pharmacists, that this little event always touched me very much.

George had been an Army Bandsman in his younger days and was a highly skilled and accomplished musician. He organised the orchestra which played for the weekly dances and was the leading performer. He told me that at every dance, during the interval, another old lady patient always came up to the platform and placed three packets of cigarettes, one neatly at each end and one in the middle, for the players. Most of them were members of the Staff, but one was a patient, so the players would pick up the cigarettes, so that the old lady could see that her gifts were appreciated, and then afterwards give them all to the one member who was a patient.

George was always late getting home after the weekly dances as they usually went on till about nine o'clock. One morning he came in with a grin all over his face and informed us that he had "a bit of a turn-up" after the dance the previous evening. It appeared that he had been on his way home after the dance and going down the long drive he saw a completely naked woman running ahead of him. He gave chase and as he came up with her she collapsed into a ditch at the side of the drive, apparently unconscious.

He hauled her out and found she was bleeding all over from scores of small flesh wounds, her only shred of covering being a torn remnant of nightdress round her neck. He slung her over his shoulder and carried her up to the hospital. There he found everything in uproar. She had just that moment been missed, and search parties were being organised to go out and look for her. It seemed that she had become very disturbed earlier in the evening and the nurse had given her a sedative and tucked her up in bed and left her quite quiet and peaceful. Being so short-staffed the nurse had been too busy with all her other patients to be able to go and look at her. After an hour or so the effect of the sedative had worn off, and the woman had jumped out of bed, seized a shoe, rushed round the ward breaking seventeen windows with the heel, climbed out through one of them, tearing her nightdress off and cutting herself all over on the broken glass, then dashed off down the drive, where George had found her.

We learned to take that sort of thing in our stride, and nothing could ruffle George.

We got a bit of amusement from the doctors sometimes. At a Mental hospital where I went frequently for a number of years there were two women doctors on the Staff, both somewhere either side of forty. One was a big-built, placid, sweet soul, much loved by the patients and popular with everybody. The other was a waspish little creature, nervy and highly strung, apt to be very irritable and bad tempered. She was a martyr to stomach ulcers and was popularly believed to subsist entirely on strong black coffee, Dexedrine, and antacid tablets. The two were bosom friends and I was quite friendly with both of them. One of my locum visits happened to coincide with a small-pox scare, and I found everyone, Staff and patients alike, being vaccinated wholesale.

A new method of vaccination had just been introduced whereby the serum was merely pressed into the epidermis by means of an appliance which we always called the "pressure-gun." I believe the method is in general use now, but at that time it was so new that the appliances were very difficult to obtain and there was only one in the entire hospital. The Staff and patients loved it, as it was completely painless, and there was no scraping or puncturing of the skin, as in the usual method of vaccination. This made a very great difference to the work of the doctors and nurses when dealing with nervous and disturbed patients, and the doctors were always trying to sneak the pressure gun and keep it for their own exclusive use. For this reason, it had to be kept under lock and key in the pharmacy, and only issued under signature to the doctor who was in charge of vaccination clinic at the time. I gathered that this method, though extremely satisfactory, did not give quite such long-term protection as the older method, but as it obviated any pain, and the results of "taking" were not as violent, it was quite understandably popular.

The only member of the Medical Staff who objected to it was our irritable Dr. Margaret. She maintained - long and loud - that vaccination could not possibly be effective unless the vaccine were introduced into the blood-stream by means of puncturing the skin, and preferably by drawing blood. Apparently, she drove the rest of the Medical Staff quite demented by her ceaseless inveighing against the new method, in season and out of season. It was noticeable, however, that when she was on vaccination duty the queues of voluntary patients - for the Staff were not compelled to be vaccinated though most of them went voluntarily - were very much smaller than when one of the other doctors was on vaccination clinic and known to be using the pressure gun. I had not been vaccinated for some years, so went along to be done, and found the use of the pressure gun quite painless and really most interesting.

One day in the pharmacy, I heard voices raised in the corridor in hot argument, then the door was thrown open and Dr. Margaret flounced in, followed by the placid Dr. Edna.

"Alright," Edna was saying, “if you insist upon my doing you by the puncture method, I'll do it. You have been screaming for blood all this time, so I'll guarantee you get blood if it's the last thing I do."

I asked mildly why they had come to the pharmacy for the performance and were not doing it in the clinic. It appeared that Margaret insisted upon having absolutely fresh vaccine, and I indignantly repudiated the suggestion that any vaccine issued to the clinic was anything other than absolutely fresh. However, Margaret peeled off her white coat and pulled one arm out of her jumper. I drew up a chair for her, and she plumped herself down, one arm on the dispensing bench, and the other extended for Edna's attentions, burying her face in the arm on the bench. I collected the necessaries and gave them to Edna. For some moments she scratched at Margaret's arm with the sterile needle I had given her, then looked up at me despairingly.

"She's got a hide like a rhinoceros," she exclaimed, "a needle is no good for her. Would you give me a scalpel blade please? I'll see what I can do with that."

"Oh, you butcher," came in a smothered howl from Margaret, "this is supposed to be a vaccination, not an amputation."

"Be quiet," said Edna severely, "you want blood, so I am going to get blood whether you like it or not."

She gave a few little snicks with the scalpel, and in a couple of minutes beads of blood appeared.

"You'd better have a look," said Edna, "and check that I really have drawn blood since you're so keen on it."

Margaret took one look at her arm, then gave a small gasp and quietly fainted. Edna caught her expertly as she slid off the chair and lowered her to the floor, while I seized and supported the treated arm. Charlie, the old porter, caught up a handful of pharmaceutical literature and slipped the sheets under her head remarking, "I ain't 'ad time to clean me floor yet, but that's no reason she should get 'er 'air full o' dust."

Edna, kneeling on the floor, sat back on her heels and looked up at me in exasperation.

"Would you believe it?" she exclaimed, "there she had been drawing blood on all her vaccination cases and driving all of us in the Common

Room up the walls, going on about it, and now when I draw a spot of blood on her own arm, out she goes like a light. We had better finish off the job at once before she comes round."

Edna and I had just completed the dressing when Margaret opened her eyes and bounced up at once.

"Lie down, you fool," said Edna, pushing her back on the floor, "you'll only pass out again if you jump up suddenly like that. Nice exhibition you have made of yourself, I must say, after all your carrying on about blood. I hope this will take good and proper and teach you what your vaccination cases have to put up with due to your out of date methods.

Margaret's arm certainly did take good and proper. Of course, the news of her downfall flashed round the hospital in no time, and everyone was in fits of laughter at her expense, especially when within a couple of days she was off duty with a high temperature, and her arm swollen up like a bolster. It was the most ferocious "take" in the whole hospital.

I went along to her room one evening after pharmacy closing time and found her in bed, her room in utter chaos, and she in a very bad temper.

"Don't you come here jeering at me," she snapped. "The entire Medical Staff has been in one time and another, and all they can do is jeer at me, and say it serves me right. They are just chortling over me, the brutes."

"I haven't any intention of jeering at you," I replied. "I have just come to see how you are and if there is anything I can do for you. I might as well tidy your bed for you first of all. It is a perfect rat's nest and does not look as if it has been made for days."

"Don't you dare touch me," she screamed, "this arm is giving me absolute hell. Home Sister tried to tidy me up, but she jumped like a rabbit when I shouted at her and shook the bed and hasn't been here since."

I took no notice of her but pulled the lower sheet taut and tidied the bed clothes, then found a brush and comb.

"Your hair doesn't look as if it had been touched for days," I said. "You look a perfect fright. You'll feel much better when I have finished with you. In any case," I went on, "I don't imagine Edna has been jeering at you, she is much too kind-hearted to do that sort of thing."

"No," said Margaret, "but she has undertaken the care of all my patients while I am out of it, and she is so busy she doesn't know which way to run first. She has only managed to look in once for about half a minute."

Margaret endured my ministrations quite meekly, and actually expressed gratitude when at last she was tidy and comfortable.

"I don't mind you handling me," she said. "Most people drive me mad. They all seem scared stiff to come near me and of course that simply makes me yell at them worse than ever."

By the time she was well enough to come back on duty again, the main wave of the small-pox scare was over, but it was noticeable that she was much more subdued and amenable than before. She and I became very good friends.

CHAPTER 14

In all I have worked at thirty-three different hospitals, of which fourteen are Mental hospitals. As is only to be expected, most of my more amusing experiences have been at Mental hospitals. There is a sameness about General hospitals and an absence of the free and easy atmosphere which I have always enjoyed so much at Mental hospitals. Also there is so much in the way of improvements and developments going on in the Mental world, and it is all so fundamentally dependent upon the innovation of new drugs and treatments, that we in the pharmacy feel we are far more an integral part of the new winds of change that are blowing throughout the Mental world, than we do in the more stereotyped world of General hospitals.

Throughout my years as full-time locum I had many repeat engagements at all the hospitals and collected a wide circle of friends. It was at one of the Mental hospitals that I first made my acquaintance with the inside of a modern prison. On one of my repeat visits I found that the Staff had got up a Concert Party among themselves. They had already given a performance for the patients, and this had proved such a success that they had been asked to repeat it in the Church Hall of the neighbouring village. Here again it had gone down so well that they received a request from the Governor of an Open Prison a few miles away that they should give the performance again for the prisoners. This had been arranged to take place a few days after my arrival and I was invited to go along as a guest. At that time the new Nurses' Home was still in process of building, and most of the Staff were accommodated in various large country houses all around the district, the hospital coach being in constant use fetching and returning them. This coach was to be used to convey all the performers to the prison and space was at a premium, so I was quite honoured to be invited to take up one of the seats.

Prior to this, the final performance, a situation had arisen which was pure Cinderella in real life. If I could not vouch for its absolute truth I should hesitate to record it, as it seems too contrived to be true.

The very evening before this performance, one of the organisers had heard a very sweet voice singing somewhere in the background purlieus behind the Staff dining room. On investigation it was found to come from a little Italian girl, quite one of the humblest members of the Staff, being nothing more than a scullery maid, spending her life washing up. She was dressed in a grubby overall with broken-down shoes, up to the elbows in greasy water, and singing like a nightingale. It was immediately decided that such a voice would have to be incorporated in the programme, and she was forthwith snatched away from her dirty crockery and dishpans, popped into a bath, her hair washed and set, after which she emerged as no longer a dirty little scrub, but a pretty, sweet-faced child with a shy manner and enchanting smile. A pretty frock was borrowed for her and there was a wild scramble round the whole female staff to find a pair of long white gloves, as her poor little hands were so red and rough that they quite spoilt the effect. It was the most perfect Cinderella transformation that one could imagine.

Transport to the prison proved a bit of a problem. Mr. Price, the Laboratory technician, was a tall, lanky individual with rough, curly, prematurely grey hair, and the lined, clever face of the typical scientist. His mind always seemed to be roaming in some exalted sphere of test tubes and complicated apparatus and pathological specimens and reagents, so it came as a surprise to find that he was a key man in the amateur orchestra. In some unimaginable corner of the cellars he had found an absolutely enormous double bass cello, quite the largest instrument of its kind that I have ever seen. How it had come to be there, how long it had been mouldering there, or how it had got there in the first place, nobody knew, but Mr. Price had extricated it from mounds of ancient rubbish, cleaned it up and restrung it, and it was now the pride and joy of his life, even ranking with his beloved laboratory and his pipe. The latter was a permanent fixture between his teeth and his head was usually surrounded by a halo of pungent smoke. The great instrument was the foundation and anchor of the entire orchestra, and Mr. Price and his double bass were absolutely essential in unifying the somewhat sketchy efforts of the other players.

But that double bass took up an enormous amount of room in the coach, and Mr. Price would not be separated from it for a moment. Musical instruments have always had a great fascination for me and realising my genuine interest in the huge beautiful thing, Mr. Price admitted me to the restricted circle of his favour actually inviting me into his laboratory and allowing me to handle it before we set off. Once in the coach, the double bass was found to be too tall to stand up, so it had to lie on its side at the far end of the centre gangway. It was suggested that it should be lashed on top of the coach, but Mr. Price would not hear of it. He and I took up strategic positions on either side, he adjuring me to see that no one kicked or tripped over the huge thing. This was none too easy, for as the coach went around from one Nurses' residence to another so we picked up more and more clusters of performers, all clutching their stage props and clamouring to get in. Eventually everybody was sitting on someone else's knee, and the centre gangway was like a tube train in the rush hour. Unfortunately, the second coach was out of commission and all available cars were in use, but the good-natured driver at last had to protest.

"I shall get into trouble for over-loading," he said. "If we go on like this I shall lose my licence and my job, and I just can't risk it."

This drew wails of complaint, and more urgent pleas.

"All right, I'll risk it," he said at length, "but you will have to play fair with me if I take you. We go through a couple of villages, and there are one or two stretches were one is apt to meet a policeman, so as soon as we get anywhere near, I shall call out 'everybody down' and all those who are sitting on people's knees, or standing up, will have to get down on the floor and under the seats, anywhere so you are out of sight, till I say you can get up again."

Everybody agreed eagerly, and off we went. An enormous coloured nurse plonked herself on my lap, billowing round me on all sides like an eiderdown and quivering all over with the giggles. The congestion was incredible. Suddenly the driver called "everybody down". How they did it no one could imagine but immediately everyone except those legitimately seated, disappeared down on the floor all among our feet, coming up a few minutes later, dishevelled, laughing and gasping for air. This was repeated several times, and Mr. Price and I had a desperate time protecting the double bass, which took up as much room on the floor as half a dozen people.

At last we drew up outside a huge, park-like entrance. The big gates had been removed also the iron railings, though there were low walls to show where they had been. We stopped at the gateway where a quiet, well-spoken man in neat dark blue battle dress, was waiting for us. He climbed in beside the driver to show him the way round the scattered complex of buildings to the Main Recreation Hall, where the performance was to take place. He was so quiet and civil that it took us a long time to realise that he was actually one of the prison inmates.

The big hall was packed to the ceiling, and seldom could a Concert Party have had a better or more appreciative audience. I found a place on one of the half dozen raised seats at the back, together with a few other guests and the senior members of the prison staff. Warders were scattered inconspicuously among the audience, but they were obviously enjoying the performance as much as the prisoners were.

It was our little Italian Cinderella who was the real hit of the evening. She completely stole the show. She was so pretty and sang so delightfully that she absolutely brought the house down. All those men positively devoured her and she was called back again and again. She looked quite bewildered at first by the warmth of her reception, then very soon overcame her shyness and smiled so enchantingly at everybody that it was no wonder she held up the whole show.

To me, however, it was Mr. Price and his double bass that held my eyes to the almost complete exclusion of everything else. He took his stance at one side of the stage, his pipe in full blast, his eyes fixed on infinity, his mind apparently completely disassociated from the activities of his huge bony hands, which flickered up and down the strings, plucking and slapping, and keeping up a faultless, inexorable rhythm, which underpinned and steadied the somewhat erratic efforts of the rest of the amateur orchestra. Occasionally his hands would skitter off in a crazy obligato of their own, of which he apparently took not the slightest notice. I simply could not take my eyes off those flickering hands, and the thumping boom of the great instrument completely hypnotised me.

After the show we were all invited to an excellent buffet supper, at which the prison inmates waited on us with the greatest friendliness and charm. This was followed by a dance, in which all our party joined with the inmates. I was too tired at the end of a day's work to take part in the dancing, which went on till quite late. The music was provided by our own orchestra supplemented by the really excellent prison orchestra. Mr. Price and his double bass were much in demand and the instrument greatly admired. I found a quiet side room and sat down for a rest. The Governor's wife, a most charming person, joined me and we spent a very pleasant time exchanging our experiences of prisons and hospitals.

Next day our little Cinderella was back at her dish-tub again, perfectly cheerful and unspoilt by all the admiration and attention of the previous evening. I have often wished that I could have heard what eventually happened to her. By the time of my next visit there, she had returned to her family in Italy and we never heard anything more about her.

It was inevitable that my endless round of locums should come to an end some time, though I could not imagine how it would come about. The demands for my services were as pressing as ever, and over the years I had built up a circuit of hospitals which kept me fully employed for as many months of the year as I cared to work. I had eliminated a number of those which I did not care for, either on account of the living conditions or the company, or because they entailed too much long-distance travelling. At one time and another I had been as far afield as Gloucestershire, Devon, Somerset, Pembrokeshire, the Midlands, Guernsey, and all round the Home Counties, as well as in London, so now I concentrated on those hospitals which were within weekend reach of home. Doc was well aware of the desperate need for my services and was quite content for me to go on as long as I liked. Without his support and co-operation, together with his complete competence in looking after himself and running the house during my prolonged absences, I should never have been able to do all the work I did. He had given me a pedometer some years before, and this I wore at my waist during working hours. At the end of each day I made a note of the mileage I had walked. It was usually between four and five miles, sometimes as much as six, and once well over seven. It must be borne in mind that this was not straight on end walking but to and fro, to and fro in the pharmacy, which is a far more exhausting business.

Though I loved the work and the active life and constant change of surroundings as much as ever, the strain began to tell at last. One day I collapsed in the pharmacy and was rushed into Staff Sick Bay.

Fortunately, there was a good and reliable assistant pharmacist whom I could leave in charge. I believe I was unconscious for twenty minutes or more and gave everybody a thorough scare. Somehow, I managed to get home next day, then followed weeks and months of such utter weakness and exhaustion as I could never have imagined. I could do nothing but lie in bed, completely inert, and often thinking, in all seriousness, that I might die at any moment through sheer lack of vitality to keep alive. The doctor could find nothing organically wrong, and no treatment could help, apart from complete and prolonged rest. Doc looked after me marvellously, and I owe more to his care and ceaseless patience that I can ever repay.

Slowly, very slowly, I fought my way up out of that awful pit, but it left me permanently weakened, and any further work was quite out of the question. It was not easy to face giving up the work I loved so much and to become accustomed to being a housewife again. However, I was years over normal retiring age, and had done fourteen years of desperately strenuous and responsible work, and I can look back on those years as being the happiest of my life.

Photo of Doc with the much loved Kikmi,
taken at Faracre, Worthing in the summer of 1937

Arthur Cecil Roper (Major)

b. 14 June 1890 (Tasmania)

d. 29 July 1978 (Worthing)

Married Frances Ann Hubbard

22 August 1933

at St Stephen's Church,

Cinderford, Gloucestershire.

MEDICINE AND MYTH

Presidential Address Given to the

Worthing Archaeological Society

by

Frances Ann Roper.

12th January 1954.

South Farm Road

Worthing.

The Art of the Physician is a far older thing than the art of the Surgeon. The ancients could, and did, perform many remarkable surgical operations, as can be seen by the trephined (1) skulls dating as far back as early Egyptian times, and the Early Bronze Age in Britain. But surgery could never be anything more than a drastic treatment, only to be adopted as a last resort, until the discovery of Anaesthetics and Antiseptics only about one hundred years ago. All operations had to be performed while the patient was fully conscious, unless Nature's own merciful anaesthetic of fainting, came to his aid. Even if the patient survived the shock of the operation, in a vast percentage of cases he died subsequently through infection of the wound, and gangrene. It is only very recently in the history of the human race that surgery has been able to develop into the amazing science that it is today.

Medicine, on the other hand, has a history as old as humankind. From the earliest times the Art of the Physician has always been closely associated with religious beliefs and held in the utmost veneration. For centuries it was known as The Art, and to this day a prescription will sometimes have the letters "s.a." written at the end. These stand for the words "secundum artem", i.e., "According to The Art", and mean that the doctor leaves the compounding of the preparation to the pharmacist, to be made up by him in accordance with the recognized methods.

The earliest records of medicine date from the Sumerian Civilisation, which has been revealed of recent years by excavations on the site of the ancient city of Ur. The Sumerians were a highly civilised people, and there can be no doubt that a Medical profession existed, as clay tablets have been discovered which have a bearing on Medicine, and a seal of a Sumerian physician who lived about 3,000 B.C. is now in the Wellcome Museum. The Sumerian civilisation was overthrown by the Babylonians in about 2,000 B.C., and the centre of culture then passed to Babylon, or Chaldea, as it is called in the Old Testament.

Prayer of Assyrian Physician to Ea, or Oannes, the deity known as "Lord of the Deep", from an Assyrian Tablet dating from about 2,500 B.C. It reads as follows:

"0, Ea, King of the Deep, see
I am the Magician, am thy slave.
March thou on my right hand,
Assist me on my left,
Add thy pure spell to mine;
Vouchsafe to me pure words
Make fortunate the utterances of my mouth,
Ordain that my decisions be happy,

Let me be blest where're I tread,
Let the man whom I now touch be blessed."

The Babylonians appear to have had a well-organised medical profession. One of the earliest Kings was named Hammurabi, and to him we owe the most ancient Code of laws in existence. Hammurabi lived about 1948 - 1905 B.C., and among many other subjects, his Code mentions laws relating to medical practice. One of the statements in the Code says:

"If the doctor shall treat a gentleman and shall open an abscess with a bronze knife, and shall preserve the eye of the patient, he shall receive ten shekels of silver. If the patient is a slave, his master shall pay two shekels of silver."

But it goes on to state that –

"if the doctor shall open an abscess with a bronze knife and shall kill the patient, or shall destroy the sight of the eye, his hands shall be cut off."

In the case of a slave the doctor is not so heavily penalized:

"He shall replace the slave with another slave."

The Babylonians were the first people to name the Signs of the Zodiac, also the nearer Planets, and as these had an immensely powerful bearing on the Art of Medicine, continuing right down to about three hundred years ago, it will be helpful to give a brief outline of their beliefs, which developed into the great art of Astrology.

From the beginning of human history down to the time of Copernicus and Galileo, in the 16th Century, it was unquestioningly believed that the earth was the centre of the universe, and that the sun, moon and planets revolved round it. The early astronomers of Babylon believed that the sun followed a path which passed through twelve constellations in the course of a year. These constellations were named as follows:

Aries	**The Ram**	**Libra**	**The Scales**
Taurus	**The Bull**	**Scorpio**	**Scorpion**
Gemini	**The Twins**	**Sagittarius**	**The Archer**
Cancer	**The Crab**	**Capricorn**	**The Goat**
Leo	**The Lion**	**Aquarius**	**The Water-carrier**
Virgo	**The Virgin**	**Pisces**	**The Fishes**

The year began in March, at the spring equinox, when the sun entered the constellation Aries. The name Zodiac is derived from the same root as the Greek word ζwσύ an animal. The seven recognised, planets were the Sun, the Moon, Mercury, Venus, Mars, Jupiter and Saturn.

The sign of the Zodiac, and the planet which was in the ascendancy at the time of a person's birth were believed to have a profound influence upon his character and fate. It was the custom for many centuries that all important persons should have their horoscopes cast, and these horoscopes were most carefully preserved, usually in the temples, so that the individuals could refer to them for guidance throughout their life.

The practice of Astrology was very widespread and prevailed throughout all the ancient civilisations of the East from the very dawn of history. It is known in countries as widely separated as Babylon, Egypt, India and China, and passed from Babylon and Egypt to

Greece, Rome, and westwards through Europe to Britain. So strongly was it established that in later times the planets were believed to have an affinity with plants and herbs and precious stones. In this way arose the system of medicine which prevailed almost unchanged down to the 17th century in England, and which still persists in strange folk-memories in country districts today. In a debased and garbled form Astrology still exists, as may be seen from the columns of many popular papers; it also exists in "lucky birth stones" and the charms and brooches, bearing the signs of the Zodiac, or their pictorial equivalent, which can be purchased at many stores.

It must be borne in mind that Astrology was an extremely serious science to the ancient peoples, and though today their system of Medicine is completely discredited, it held absolute sway over the greatest minds in the world for over four thousand years. It is not for us to jeer at them.

The Babylonians, or Chaldeans, were so famous for their powers of Astrology, that they held great authority in other nations, and were well known in Egypt and highly respected at the courts of the Pharaohs. From the Babylonians the knowledge passed to the Egyptians and was welded on their own theology.

Thoth, the Egyptian god of wisdom, represented with the head of an ibis, is said to have been the author of treatises on medicine. He is believed to have written thirty-two books, known as the Hermetic Books, of which six dealt with medicine. These books were kept in the temples for reference, and carried in processions, and regarded with the utmost veneration. All are now lost, but all the surviving Egyptian medical literature appears to have been compiled from these lost Hermetic Books. They were so highly esteemed that no physician was blamed for a patient's death as long as he had adhered strictly to their teachings. If, however, the physician departed in the slightest degree from those teachings, and the patient died, the physician's own life was forfeited.

The Ebers papyrus is the best known of medical papyri. It was found in a tomb at Thebes in 1862 by Professor Georg Ebers and is the oldest complete medical book in existence. It is also believed to be the oldest existing book of any kind. It consists of 110 pages and contains about 900 recipes or prescriptions. As it is in almost perfect condition, and has a calendar written at the back of the M.S. the date of its writing may be fairly accurately fixed at about 1,500 B.C. There are marginal notes made by its original owner, such as *"Good. I have often used it,"* or *"An excellent remedy."* The directions for use were to repeat while taking the mixture such words as *"Welcome, remedy! Welcome! that dost drive away that which is in this my heart and in these my limbs."* Castor oil and hartshorn are two drugs mentioned in the Ebers papyrus which are still in use today.

Horus was the Egyptian god of health. While engaged in a fight with Set, the god of evil, Horus lost an eye, which was restored by miraculous means. Representations of the Eye of Horus came to be regarded as the most potent of amulets and is believed to be the original of the PX which appears at the top of all prescriptions down to the present day. In Roman times this amulet came to be merged with the sign of Jupiter. Still later it came to be understood as the initial letter of the word "Recipe" meaning "Take thou", being directions to the compounder of the following mixture. The "R" however, always has a line through the tail, and it is strange to think that the National Health Service is unwittingly invoking the aid of Horus and Jupiter by printing the PX at the head of their official prescription forms.

The earliest physician whose name is known is Sekhet-eanach who was chief physician to one of the Pharaohs about 3,000 B.C. All that is known of him is that "he healed the King's nostrils." The second name, and one much better known, is that of Im-Hotep, which means, "he who cometh in peace." He flourished about 2,980 B.C. and was a famous politician and architect, as well as physician. He was the architect and designer of the Step Pyramid of Sakkarah. Little is known of Im-Hotep as physician, but he must have been very distinguished, for he was worshipped for many centuries after his death as the god of medicine. In later centuries he was identified by the Greeks with their own god Æsculapius.

The torch of Medicine now passes to Greece. Æsculapius is believed to have had two daughters, Hygeia and Panacea. Hygeia became the goddess of Health, and her name is still remembered in our word "hygiene". The name of Panacea is still used to indicate any preparation which is believed to cure all ills.

Serpents have always been connected with the Art of Medicine, and there is a vast amount of literature dealing with the cult of the Serpent. The most obvious reason for the ancient belief is that the serpent casts its skin and reappears apparently rejuvenated. This led to the belief that serpents had the power of renewing their youth and health, and from the most ancient times they have been looked upon as the symbol of healing. A gold and ivory statuette of a Minoan Priestess holding two serpents, has been found, dating from an extremely early period. Serpents came to be connected with this name Æsculapius, and still appears in the badge of the Royal Army Medical Core.

In the year 460 B.C. in the little island of Cos near the coast of Asia Minor, was born one of the greatest men the world has ever known - Hippocrates, the Father of Medicine. He is said to have been a direct descendant of Æsculapius.

Until the time of Hippocrates, the study of Medicine had been entirely empirical, and without any scientific basis whatever. All sickness and disease was believed to be the work of devils or malevolent gods, for many centuries had yet to pass before the discovery of germs. All treatments were strictly in accordance with the accepted codes, and the nature of the diseases was not studied at all. Many of the standard treatments were determined by the study of the stars and their corresponding herbs. Hippocrates however, originated an entirely different school of thought. He based his teachings upon careful and intensive study of the patient, and set a high standard for all who wished to follow what he called The Art. He set the pattern of ethical conduct, insistence on prognosis, accuracy of observation and clarity in recording of cases which has remained unsurpassed to this day. He wrote many works on the Art of Medicine, some of which were used. as textbooks till the beginning of the nineteenth century. His famous "Aphorisms" or short definitions and advice to students, are as true and fresh today as when he wrote them nearly two thousand years ago. The famous Oath of Hippocrates has been adopted as a pattern by medical men throughout the ages, and in one form or another has been taken by thousands of doctors when achieving their qualification. In this noble code of ethics, the student is shown the dignity and responsibility of his calling, and there is urged upon him the duty of respect to his school or university, of making any new discovery freely available, of 'maintaining professional secrecy and refraining from gossip, and of taking no mean advantage of the position of medical advisor. Upon this has been based the high standards which have characterised the medical profession to this day.

<u>Extracts from one of the renderings of The Oath of Hippocrates</u>

"I swear by Apollo the Physician, by Æsculapius, by Hygeia,by Panacea, and by all the gods and goddesses, making them my witnesses, that I will carry out according to my ability and judgement, this oath and this indenture. . . . . I will use treatment to help the sick

according to my ability and judgement, but never with a view to injury and wrongdoing. Neither will I administer a poison to anybody when asked to do so, nor will I suggest such a course. . . . But I will keep pure and holy both my life and my art. Into whatsoever houses I enter, I will enter to help the sick, and I will abstain from all wrongdoing and harm, especially from abusing the bodies of man or woman, bond or free. And whatsoever I shall hear in the course of my profession, as well as outside my profession in my intercourse with men, if it be what should not be published abroad, I will never divulge, holding such things to be holy secrets. Now if I carry out this oath and break it not, may I gain for ever reputation among all men for my life and for my art; but if I transgress it and forswear myself, may the opposite befall me."

Extracts from the "Precepts of Hippocrates."

"I urge you not to be too grasping, but to consider carefully your patient's means. Sometimes give your services for nothing... and if there be an opportunity of serving one who is a stranger in financial straits, give full assistance to all such. For where there is the love of man, there is also love of the art."

Hippocrates has made little use of drugs. His method was to watch the course of the disease and to assist nature's own power of recuperation. Unlike the vast majority of early medical writers, he had the wisdom and humility to record his failures as well as his successes, and so well and accurately did he record his cases that the diseases are easily recognizable today. Cases of malaria, meningitis, and the laboured breathing known as Cheyne-Stokes respiration can be recognized among others. Hippocrates lived to a great age, and is believed to have died in 355 B.C.

If the medical world had followed and developed the wide and sane teachings of Hippocrates, knowledge would have advanced far more rapidly than it did, and thousands of sufferers throughout the centuries would have been spared untold miseries. But Hippocrates lived before his time, and his teachings were far too advanced for the world in its then state. After his death the medical world quickly relapsed into the old condition of superstition and magical beliefs, and wildly inaccurate guess-work from which Hippocrates had done so much to raise it.

As the Grecian Culture declined, so the Roman culture arose. Great Medical Schools were founded in various places, the most famous of which was at Alexandria. There were many teachers of medicine during the next four and a half centuries, but after Hippocrates the man who left the greatest mark on the world of medicine was Galen. He was born in Asia Minor in 131 A.D. and studied at Alexandria. He was a very different type from Hippocrates, and it is mainly due to his self-opinionated and didactic temperament and methods of teaching, that he attained the enormous influence which he wielded throughout the medical world for the next 1,300 years. Galen was extremely active and contentious, and though he had no definite followers nor did he establish any school, his reputation during his lifetime was prodigious, and he left a voluminous collection of writings. On his death in 200 A.D. all active research ceased absolutely. A black curtain descends upon the world of medicine, the great Library of Alexandria was destroyed, the Dark Ages of Medicine began, and the works and teachings of Galen became fossilised and venerated, till they loomed over the minds of men as a lowering monolith, which none might question on pain of death. To this day certain standard preparations are still known as "Galenicals." (2)

During the succeeding centuries the teachings of Galen became more and more overgrown with superstition and myth. The ancient beliefs of Astrology reared their heads once more, till at last by the beginning of the fourteenth century the Medical world was in a state of chaos. During those dark centuries the only points of light in the western world were the Monasteries and other Church Institutions. The monks became considerably skilled in the use of herbs and simple remedies and grew many of the medicinal plants in the Monastic gardens. These medicinal herbs and plants are still found growing wild on the sites and among the ruins of ancient Abbeys and Monasteries. Belladonna has been found in the ruins of Kinross Abbey, and at Valle Crusis Abbey, Llangollen. Henbane and Datura Stramonium have also been found quite recently and are obviously the descendants of the medicinal herb gardens of the monks.

Numbers of the herbal drugs used by the Mediaeval physician are still in use. The common fox-glove, broom, dandelion, monkshood (aconite), chamomile, peppermint, horseradish, belladonna, colchicum (autumn crocus), hyoscyamus (henbane), fern root, witch hazel, linseed, are all indigenous plants which have been used for centuries and are still in use today. Some are falling out of use due to the discovery of new synthetic drugs, but many are in common use and have no substitutes.

One of the strange beliefs which came down from very early times was that of the "Doctrine of Signatures". Briefly this meant that certain signs, forms and shapes existed in plants and animals, which indicated their powers and virtues in the healing of diseases. It was an ingenious system for discovering from certain marks and appearances in the various portions of a plant's structure, the medicinal properties it possessed. It is probable that this doctrine was evolved from the curious resemblances to be observed between the leaves, flowers and roots of certain plants and various parts of the human body. The most potent plant in this category was considered in ancient times to be the mandrake, on account of the bifurcated root, which bears some resemblance to the human body. Many superstitions arose concerning the mandrake, it was believed to be so nearly human that it screamed when pulled out of the ground, and the person who pulled it up was in great danger of insanity or even death. The mandrake does actually contain a certain amount of a known poison (probably Scopolamine) and it induced hallucinations and temporary mental derangement. In order to obtain the root, and yet to escape the dangers attendant upon actually pulling it up, the ingenious method was devised by which a dog was tied to the loosened root, so that the attendant disasters should fall upon the dog, and not upon the person concerned. The Herbarium of Apuleius (5th cent. A.D.) gives the following directions for gathering Mandrake:

"When thou seest its hands and its feet, then tie thou it up. Take the other end and tie it to a dog's neck, so that the hound be hungry; next cast meat before him, so that he may not reach it, except he jerk up the wort with him."

There are many Mediaeval illustrations showing a dog tethered to the mandrake root.

Shakespeare often refers to mandragora and its effects.

"Give me to drink mandragora. . .

That I might sleep out this great gap of time my Antony is away".

(Antony and Cleopatra I v.4.)

"And shrieks like mandrakes torn out of the earth

that living mortals hearing them, run mad."

(Romeo and Juliet IV iii. 47).

The plant cyclamen was used for ear complaints, because the leaf resembles the human ear. Spotted plants were administered to cure spots, and scaly plants to remove scaly disorders of the skin. The little blue speedwell, which resembles a bright blue eye, was also known as "eye-bright" and was used for disorders of the eyes. The flowers of the Canterbury bell, which look like an open throat, were used for bronchitis. The list may be continued to a great length, but it is safe to say that every plant which has a common name which includes some part of the body, such as liver-wart, lung-wort, hound's-tongue, hart's-tongue etc., was used in ancient times for the part of the body named.

Another strange belief was that of Healing by Sympathy. It appears by present standards to be a most wild and fantastic theory, but it was widely held and accredited even down to the seventeenth century and advocated by intellectual people such as Sir Kenelm Digby and Madame de Sevigne, among many others. The basis of the idea was that certain ills of the body, chiefly wounds, could be cured by applying the remedy to the object which caused the injury, and not to the injury itself. Thus, if a person were wounded by a dagger, the dagger was bound up with unguents and drugs, while the actual wound was merely treated by being washed and wrapped up in clean linen. The cures which were attributed to this treatment obviously had nothing to do with the drugs used, but it was an excellent method of treatment in as far as the wound was kept clean and left to Nature, without the application of the weird, and often appalling, medicaments of the time, which almost invariably did far more harm than good.

Among the many strange beliefs which arose during the long period of darkness and superstition, one of the strongest was that of "Touching for the King's Evil". Early chroniclers declare that the healing touch was a prerogative peculiar to the sovereigns of England. The first records are by William of Malmesbury, who states that Edward the Confessor (1042-1066) was the first ruler to practice it, and the power descended by hereditary right to all succeeding sovereigns. The power was believed to be vested in one of the jewels in Edward the Confessor's Crown, and to pass to each successive rightful wearer. The disease with which the healing was chiefly associated was Scrofula, which was very common in England from the Middle Ages down to the seventeenth century and was mainly due to malnutrition. This came to be known as "The King's Evil". The power of healing was the sole right of the English sovereigns, though certain of the French Kings claimed the right, which gave rise to bitter controversy in former times. English chroniclers maintained that the French Kings only derived their power from their alliance to the English Royal line, though the French Kings continued to exercise the rite down to 1776.

A special form of religious service was instituted in the reign of Henry VII and was included in the English Prayer Book till 1719. Queen Elizabeth I disliked the practice, but she is reputed to have touched a great number of people. The Stuart sovereigns practised the healing touch, and Charles I is said by contemporary writers to have excelled all his predecessors in the exercise of the Divine gift. After the Restoration, multitudes of people flocked to London to be healed by the Royal Touch, and Charles II was indefatigable in his performance of the rite. This may have been due to the suspension of the rite during the commonwealth, although it is stated by a contemporary writer that *"that method had been tried by the late usurper Cromwell, but without success."*

Charles II touched several thousands of suffers every year, and in 1682 he performed the rite on 8,500 people. Registers were kept of every person who had been touched, and the whole thing became a well-organised public ceremony. Between the years 1660 to 1664 the total of persons touched was 23,601, and from 1667 to 1684 the numbers had increased to 68,506. So great was the increase in the number of applicants that metal tokens of copper or brass were issued by way of "tickets", and when applying for these tokens the patients had to produce certificates signed and sealed by their ministers or church-wardens, declaring that they had never previously been touched by the King. The performance of the ceremony was preceded by a Royal Proclamation, and usually took place on Good Friday, at the Palace of Westminster. The two great diarists, Pepys and Evelyn, both mention the ceremony, and give careful and interesting descriptions. It would seem that history has made a great deal of the faults of Charles 11, and not enough of his kind-heartedness and obvious sympathy with his suffering subjects, for it must have been an extremely unpleasant matter for the sovereign to have to touch the loathsome sores which were presented to him in such numbers. It is also recorded by the great contemporary scholar, Elias Ashmole, that:-

"a man named Evans, who was in such a loathsome condition that none could be found willing to recommend him for a certificate, placed himself in St. James' Park where he knew the King walked. Upon his approach he fell on his knees exclaiming, 'God bless your Majesty'. Whereupon the King gave him his hand to kiss, upon which Evans availed himself of the opportunity to apply it to his dreadfully ulcerated nose, which from that time improved and ultimately recovered."

William of Orange considered the rite a "silly superstition" and could only be persuaded to perform the ceremony once, when he remarked to the patients "God give you better health and more sense." Queen Anne revived the practice and performed the rite in London and Oxford. One of those touched by her was Samuel Johnson when about two or three years of age. The original token, or touch-piece given to him by the Queen is now in the British Museum. The Hanoverian monarchs discontinued the ancient rite, though the Young Pretender

Charles Edward, and his brother, the Cardinal of York, both continued it, and special silver touch-pieces were struck for them.

Another strange power with which British Sovereigns were accredited was that of Hallowing the Rings. From the earliest times rings of all kinds have been used as amulets for the cure of all kinds of diseases, but those hallowed by British Monarchs were believed to be particularly efficacious against Cramp and Epilepsy. These rings were made of any kind of metal not necessarily of gold though many which were hallowed for foreign rulers or wealthy persons were of gold or silver. The majority were of iron, lead or bronze, and rings made of nails from coffins that had been buried and exhumed, were considered particularly potent. The earliest record of a British monarch hallowing Cramp rings is of Edward II (1307-1327), and there are many records thereafter down to the 16th century. The Hallowing of the Rings was a very solemn ceremony, conducted with a set form of prayer. The rings to be hallowed were placed in dishes before the Crucifix, and the sovereign consecrated them by passing them to and fro between his hands, so that the Royal Virtue might impregnate them. These consecrated rings were in very great demand in all countries, for though the French kings claimed the power of Touching, no person in the world was credited with the power of Hallowing the Rings other than the reigning Sovereign of England. Very few of these Cramp Rings are now in existence, though there are frequent allusions to them in chronicles and records from widely separated sources.

Jewels and precious stones have always ranked very nigh among the objects employed for their believed powers of healing. Each of the planets was believed to rule and influence its own precious stones in the same way that it influenced its own plants. Good spirits were supposed to reside in certain stones and to exert their beneficent powers upon the wearer. Jewels were frequently worn as amulets and were also powdered and given internally as medicines. The widespread belief during the Middle Ages in the healing powers and curative action of precious stones is shown in the medical formularies and Pharmacopoeias of the period, many of which continued in use till as recently as 1798. A compound called "Hungary Powder" of that period was renowned as a remedy for smallpox and measles and was given in doses of 20-30 grains. Among a number of other ingredients, it contained powdered emeralds, rubies, sapphires, jacinths, pearls, red and white coral, and gold leaf. The great cost of the gems used in these compounds led naturally to the apothecaries substituting artificial stones for genuine ones, so during the seventeenth and eighteenth centuries these costly ingredients gradually went out of use.

The belief that toads carried a jewel in their heads is a very ancient one, but its origin is lost in myth and legend. The "jewel" was believed to have immense therapeutic value for all kinds of ailments, and the method of obtaining it from the living toad is carefully recorded. It was necessary to get an old, male toad, and place it on a piece of scarlet material. This colour so pleased the toad, that it would stretch itself out, wriggling with delight, and open its mouth and eject the jewel. It was, however, very important that the observer should watch the toad very closely, as directly it had ejected the jewel, it would appear to realise the enormity of its action, and, unless the jewel were snatched away immediately, the toad would at once "sup it up" again and refuse ever after to relinquish it.

The influence of the Renaissance was as potent in the world of Medicine as in every other sphere of life, but it was very largely due to the activities of that strange, paradoxical, yet brilliant and original thinker, Philippus Aureolus Theophrastus Bombastus von Hohenheim, self-styled Paracelsus (1490-1541) that the centuries-old bondage of Galen began to break. The Medical world had become ossified and petrified, bound down and shackled under a mountainous and stifling welter of theory and legend, whose foundation was the immutable teaching of Galen.

Paracelsus whirled into the hidebound theorists of his period like a tornado, and naturally drew down upon his head all the weight of disapproval and denunciation of which they were capable. He needed every ounce of his natural self-confidence and braggadocio to withstand the furious onslaughts of the established members of the profession. For many years Paracelsus has been decried as a charlatan, a mere drunken quack, and a disreputable braggart, and it is quite probable that he fully merited those terms. But it is only of recent years that students have begun to appraise him at his real worth. He was a born Iconoclast, and the whole subsequent development of the Medical Profession is deeply indebted to him for his brilliant work in blazing the trail which has led to the marvels of modern Medical knowledge.

With Paracelsus and the Renaissance, the structure of modern Medicine can be said to have begun. In following the trail so violently blazed by Paracelsus, Medicine has found that the trail leads back unerringly to that greatest of all Physicians, Hippocrates. With the advance of modern Medicine Hippocrates has, after nearly 2,500 years, at last come into his own. His precepts are as true and fresh today as they were when he first taught them, and his is the abiding and underlying spirit which imbues and irradiates the whole profession, however encrusted it may become with technicalities, or dehumanised by the Welfare State.

The old mediaeval beliefs died hard, and even today many queer beliefs still linger as mere whispers of folk memories in out-of-the-way districts. Many of the names of drugs and preparations in the British Pharmacopoeia are still traceable to those early times, and many others still crop up in common parlance, frequently to the headache and annoyance of the youthful pharmacist. Certain popular items may have as many as three or four different names, apart from their official name, and the names may vary in different parts of the country. But despite the inconvenience to the trained professional, these names are of the very stuff and substance of our history, and to those who have eyes to see and ears to hear, they echo back to those far-off days when the Art of the Physician was indeed a mystery and inspired by God.

1. Trepanning, also known as trepanation, trephination, trephining or making a burr hole is a surgical intervention in which a hole is drilled or scraped into the human skull, exposing the dura mater to treat health problems related to intracranial diseases or release pressured blood build-up from an injury.

2. Galenicals medicines made of natural rather than synthetic components.

Trick of the Trade

By Frances Ann Roper

When it became known that Professor Langham was planning a 'dig' on the South Downs, a ripple of excitement spread throughout the archaeological world. For several summers prior to 1939 he had conducted excavations on some of the prehistoric hill forts, and the results of his researches had had far-reaching effects in erudite circles. The workers were mostly drawn from among his own students, and he had gathered a small band of trained assistants who helped with the organisation and instruction. Naturally the 'digs' had had to be abandoned during the war years, and the little nucleus of trained assistants had been scattered to the winds. Now, at last, he had been able once more to get a party of students together, and some half dozen of the old gang as ballast.

After high tea on the first evening of camp the Professor beat upon the trestle table with a spoon for silence and rose to make an announcement. As his six feet odd of endless bony frame unwound itself and towered into the roof of the marquee almost above the range of the hurricane lamps set at intervals down the tables, a sonorous and most beautiful voice from the level of the Professor's elbow intoned, "My Lords, Ladies and Gentlemen, budding Archaeologists, and all other variegated scum, pray silence for the most Worshipful and Venerable ……."

The chant was cut short by an imploring whisper from the Professor. “Armitage, for heaven's sake, don’t be more of a fool than you can help. Haven't you grown up at all during the last seven years?”

Silence being at last secured, the Professor looked round the marquee, where at long tables were gathered some forty or fifty students, all clad in the most amazing selection of camp attire. He himself looked very unlike the long-dignified figure in gown and mortarboard so familiar to the majority of the students. Huge hobnailed boots with rough socks turned down over them were continued upwards by incredibly long bony legs, these in turn sketchily clad in chalk-stained corduroy shorts. Above this came a disgracefully shabby suede wind-cheater, the whole surmounted by a magnificent head and face that might have served as model for Durer’s portrait of Erasmus. In his best lecture-hall voice the Professor outlined the scheme of work for the next few weeks and gave a brief and dignified welcome to the half dozen or so foreign students who had, at the request of their various Universities, come to study English methods of excavation.

“I will now ask the old gang to come along to my tent while we work out the teams. All others are free for the rest of the evening. Cocoa and buns will be served at the cook-house at half past nine, and all lights out in tents at ten-thirty.”

“And no scuffling over cocoa and buns either,” appended the same beautiful voice that had interrupted before. “You'll all form up and parade in threes or I’ll know the reason why.”

"Must you really play the goat, Armitage?" pleaded the Professor. "How are we ever going to get any discipline in this camp if you insist on fooling all the time?"

"Sorry, Big Chief," grinned the offender. "It is simply youthful joie-de-vivre at being in camp again after all these years."

Armitage, dark and saturnine, possessed of a voice of the most amazing charm, and an astonishing pair of Mephistophelean eyebrows, was an erstwhile student of the Professor's, and one of his most competent and highly trained assistants; and incidentally his most devoted henchman and admirer. An ex-Captain of Commandos he had now returned to his pre-war job of junior Science Lecturer at the Professor's college.

The old gang adjourned to the bell tent which was the Professor's bedroom and study, as well as the centre for all the archaeological stores: innumerable paper bags for specimens and 'finds,' boxes of labels, bundles of pegs of all sizes, tins, steel tapes, tools of all sorts and kinds, in fact such a heterogeneous collection that the human beings could hardly find any unoccupied spot on which to dispose themselves.

Besides the Professor and Armitage, the old gang comprised Colonel and Mrs. Enderby, Baxter, Hardcastle, and Wilkinson.

The Colonel, a lawyer in civilian life, had spent seven years in the Army, ending up by taking a responsible part on the War Crimes Commission. He was a large and powerfully built man, an indefatigable worker, and the Professor's close friend and right-hand man. His capacity for tireless work had led to Armitage's famous remark – "If you see a hole in the Downs and a non-stop jet of rubble flying out of it, you can be certain Enderby is at the bottom."

Baxter was a small, anxious person, too frail and short-sighted to have taken any active part in war service. He had, however, developed into one of the most outstanding experts in Radar research. Despite this, he was almost too nervous to raise his voice above a whisper, and his admiration for Enderby and Armitage was touching in its humility. Wilkinson was a tough and virile individual, games coach in civilian life, P.T. Instructor in the R.A.F. during the war, and now back at his old job once more. Hardcastle was a gentle, apparently dreamy soul, junior librarian at the same college as the Professor. To everyone's astonishment he had blossomed out into a fighter pilot of outstanding brilliance and had now returned happily to his beloved library with the rank of Squadron Leader and several decorations to his credit.

Alison Enderby was the only woman in the old gang and had been accepted as one of themselves from the first. Small and fragile in appearance, she usually wore an expression of wide-eyed innocence, which masked a brain equal to that of any of the men for keenness, linked with a devastating quickness of intuition and insight which often left the men gasping. During the pre-war camps each one of the old gang excepting perhaps the Professor, had laid his broken heart at her feet, only to have it restored to the owner with a grace and air of surprised gratitude which went far towards re-establishing balance and mutual respect. She was far happier and more at ease in the company of men than of women and had that rare gift of listening which made her a beloved and welcome member of the gang. In her slim fingers lay all the wizardry of the pencil; hers was the responsibility for preparing all the multitudinous drawings, plans, sections and sketches which form so vitally important a part of an archaeological dig.

The old gang had not forgathered in its entirety since the dramatic dig in the summer of 1939, when the camp had been summarily broken up by the Army commandeering all their equipment on the spot. So, for an hour or so the talk shuttled back and forth across the lamp-lit tent: news, reminiscences to be exchanged, and threads to be picked up.

Presently Wilkinson asked, "Did you see any active service, Professor?"

The Professor looked coyly down his nose. "I was in the Home Guard," he replied with an air of modest worth, "and I was a corporal for a short time."

A roar of delight made the tent pole rock.

"Our Professor was a corporal in the Home Guard," chanted Armitage. "Our Professor with more brains in his little finger than all the rest of us put together – he was a corporal in the Home Guard."

"Why only for a short time Professor?" asked someone.

The Professor looked positively sheepish. "We were out on manoeuvres on the Downs," he replied. "I knew every inch of the area, so was deputed to act as guide to our side. I was crawling up a steep slope on my – ahem – waistcoat, when I found my nose in a rabbit scratch, and I saw that that rabbit scratch was full of fragments of Bronze Age pottery." The Professor's eyes shone behind his thick glasses. "Think of it!" he exclaimed, "Bronze Age Pottery in that area where never a trace of it had been found before. Naturally I became so enthralled that I forgot all about the manoeuvres and the next thing I became aware of was whistles blowing and my name being shouted in rather rude and uncivil tones. To cut a long and rather painful story short – I found my platoon had gone far ahead of me and become embroiled with the opposing troops. They had then fraternized in the most reprehensible manner at the nearest pub, and finally had all broken off and returned home without having been given any authorization whatever to do so."

By this time his hearers were in helpless convulsions of laughter.

"Go on Professor," gasped Armitage, "tell us what happened when your C.O. heard of it."

"I would really prefer not to recall that interview too vividly," replied the Professor primly. "It was painful in the extreme, and I was demoted on the spot."

"Who was your C.O.?" asked Colonel Enderby. He was a silent soul in general, but the Professor's recital had reduced even him to suppressed chuckles.

"Sad to say," replied the Professor, "he was not the type of person who would in any way appreciate the importance of my discovery. He was concerned solely with the manoeuvres, which by comparison with the discovery of Bronze Age pottery in that area, were matters of no moment whatever. I attempted to explain this to him, but his language became so abusive that I desisted. I believe that in private life he was a chief bartender at the Hotel Magnifique, so perhaps I could hardly expect him to view my position with anything approaching sympathetic comprehension."

"And what about Mrs. Enderby?" he went on, in the fatherly tones which always roused her ire. "Have you been keeping the home fires burning while the Colonel has been away this last few years?"

"Home fires burning my foot," was the brisk retort. "I haven't had any time to waste on domesticity. I had two years in the A.T.S. till I was discharged on medical grounds, and since then I have been back at my old job again."

"What's that?"

"Pharmacy – medicine dispensing in hospital," she replied. "I was qualified before I married and did several years in hospital, but things have advanced so rapidly this last few years that I found it a bit of a strain to pick it all up again. I haven't touched a pencil for ages," she went on, spreading her hands out in the lamp-light and examining them dismally. "I wonder if I have forgotten how to draw."

"You'd better hadn't," observed Armitage severely. "What is going to happen to the dig if we haven't got our Mrs. Enderby to do the drawings for us?"

"Now about fixing the teams," said the Professor, producing a list of names. "I shall want a good hefty team on that south rampart. It will be a hundred and twenty foot cutting at least."

"Enderby's job, obviously," said Armitage, "and I suggest he has all those Scandinavian students. They look a husky lot and good for a bit of solid work."

The foreign students comprised an assortment of huge, fair young Nordics, one or two of whom were Dutch, a couple of Danes, and the rest either Norwegians or Swedes.

Enderby groaned. “I shall never know one from the other,” he complained, “and as for sorting out their names –. Besides,” he went on, “I have been speaking German for months past, and if I come out with a bit of German to a Dutchman or Norwegian, my name is going to be mud.”

“Why worry?” said Armitage cheerfully. “Just call them Hi-you and stick to English. They’ll understand soon enough.”

Next morning work started in full swing. Enderby and his team of huskies got down to the main cutting, Armitage and a team of senior schoolboys started a nice little cutting on the west rampart, Baxter and the girl students started a nice little hut site, and the rest of the old gang, each with his own team were appointed to their several jobs. Alison Enderby annexed two budding surveyors aged about 18 and 19, and armed with drawing board, steel tapes, chains and theodolite, spent her time moving backwards and forwards over the whole area, making out the preliminary ground plan. The down-land sun blazed in a sky of dull steel blue, pierced and fretted with the filigree of the larks’ song.

At eleven came the welcome sound of the whistle, announcing the arrival of Bert Betts with a huge tin of sandwiches. Betts senior was porter at the Professor’s college, an ex-Navy cook. His joy in life was to spend his holidays running any camp of which the Professor was in charge. He saw to all the catering and cooking and, together with Mrs. Betts and a variegated assortment of junior Bettses, undertook all responsibility on the domestic side.

Being of a large and solid build, Betts himself never scaled the giddy heights of the Downs to the excavations, preferring to busy himself in the sheltered field in the valley where the camp was set up, but there was always some junior Betts available for carrying up the elevenses and the midday lunch.

The workers flung themselves down on the slopes of the northern rampart in any available spot of shade, the old gang as usual congregating a little apart.

"Well," and how are the teams working out?" asked the Professor, who had spent most of his time flitting from one to the other, superintending everything. "How are you and your huskies getting on with the main cutting?" He turned to Enderby.

The huge man stretched prodigiously. "Amazing lot of workers," he replied, "they'd cut their way through anything, but one or two are shockingly ham-handed. I shall have to watch them when we get down to anything in the way of post-holes or finds, or they'll wreck everything before I can stop them. Why, one of them nearly put the end of his pick through my skull this morning."

Alison was up in arms at once. "For heaven's sake, Doc, be careful," she exclaimed. "I have only just got you back home again and I won't have any blond beast putting his pick through your skull. Which of them was it?"

"Haven't the remotest idea," he replied lazily. "I haven't begun to get them sorted out yet. That's the worst of fair men," he added, with a glance at the saturnine Armitage, "they all look so alike."

Armitage smirked revoltingly. He was looking more piratical than ever with a red handkerchief tied round his head and his dark skin already deepening to a rich mahogany. “There’s one thing about it,” he observed, “you needn’t fear that Mrs. Enderby will go and fall for your Nordic types. Look at what she chose.” Enderby was if anything, darker than Armitage.

But Alison would not be drawn. “I mean it Doc,” she insisted. “You must find out who is the clumsy one and give him a good choking off. If you won’t, I will.”

During the next few days Enderby noticed that picks swung perilously near his head, and once, as the cutting deepened a heavy chalk block missed him by a fraction, but it was always impossible to spot the offender, and sooner than alarm Alison he made no mention of it.

The Enderbys had their tent at the far end of the camp, somewhat apart from the rest. The Professor had his right in the middle whence he could keep an eye on everything. It was Enderby’s habit to make his way each morning at about six o'clock, down the long lines of tents to the cookhouse at the opposite end of the field, where the faithful Betts had an invariable tray of tea awaiting him. The Enderbys were specially favoured as old Betts had a very soft spot for Mrs. Enderby, and Mrs. Betts an equally soft spot for the Colonel. No one else, not even the Professor, was favoured by early morning tea.

About the beginning of the second week of camp Alison awoke one morning with that strange sense of the hour being later than usual, even before looking at her watch. For a moment she lay still expecting to hear the familiar swish of her husband's gumboots through the dew-thick grass, accompanied by the cheering little rattle of the tea tray; then with a sudden jerk she sat upright looking across the tent to the other camp bed. It was twenty past six, and Enderby lay in a horribly twisted position, his long limbs flung about like those of some huge rag doll. As Alison bent over him she noticed his eyelids and lips were blue, and as she lifted his hand she saw the nails were of the same livid colour. Pressing her fingers on the great sun-tanned wrist, she found the pulse beats followed a definite and quite peculiar rhythm, and something clicked at the back of her brain, claiming registration in the conscious mind. This was no time for registering sub-conscious brain-clicks, however; Alison tugged on gumboots and mackintosh over her pyjamas and hurried down through the camp to the Professor's tent. In response to her urgent scratching at the canvas, and low-voiced calls, the Professor stuck out his head, like a tortoise from its shell, blinking in the low rays of the early sun.

"Do come, Professor," whispered Alison. "Doc seems awfully ill. I don't know what to make of it."

In a few moments he joined her at Enderby's bedside. "I will send young Bart for the doctor at once," he said after a cursory examination of his friend. "No," he amended, "I don't want to alarm anyone. I'll get Armitage to go and tell him to keep it to himself."

In a few moments Alison saw Armitage flying toward the village on his bicycle, his battered old blazer thrown over his pyjamas, and his feet thrust into ancient tennis shoes.

During, the terrible time of waiting for the doctor's arrival, the sub-conscious hammer kept beating in Alison's brain, beating through ever nearer and nearer into her consciousness. Somewhere – somehow – she had read or heard of just such symptoms as had developed in her husband; her sub-conscious mind knew all about it, but she must wait till it could break through into her brain. Grasping her husband's wrist once more, she jotted down the pulse rhythm in a series of dots and dashes. The awareness of this sub-conscious knowledge, and the inability to register it, added to her anxiety about Enderby, drew on every ounce of Alison's reserve of self-control.

The doctor proved to be a kindly and sympathetic soul, but Alison's hospital experience told her that he was not very well up in the latest therapeutic developments.

"It is obviously a form of poisoning," he said, "but what exactly it is I can't say. Has anyone else in the camp shown anything similar?"

"Not a sign of anything," said the Professor, who had already checked up. "We all had the same for dinner last night and the Colonel had not been out of camp or eaten anything apart from what we have all had." Alison nodded corroboration.

The doctor looked worried. "I am sorry to have to suggest it," he said, "but this is such a peculiar case, and so completely outside my sphere, that I should feel much happier if I could call in the advice of the police. Dr. Hannaford does most of their work, and I should be glad for him to see the case. In the meantime," he turned to Alison, "you have no need to worry. Your husband has a magnificent constitution and will probably be quite himself again in a few days' time."

The students were dispatched to the excavations under the charge of Hardcastle and Wilkinson. Presently the police Inspector arrived, accompanied by Dr. Hannaford. The doctor examined Enderby very carefully. The peculiar pulse rhythm was already fading and giving place to the regular beats. Alison gave the doctor the slip of paper on which she had recorded the rhythm, and he put it carefully away.

"This is definitely a case of poisoning," he said, "but what exactly the nature of the poison can be it is extremely difficult to tell."

As he spoke the sub-conscious knowledge sprang through into Alison's brain. In common with all pharmacists she was a weekly recipient of a startlingly erudite publication which contains information on all the latest and most abstruse research into the labyrinths of chemicals, vaccines, viruses and drugs of all sorts, and is completely incomprehensible to the layman; and largely to the average member of the profession. It is, however, printed on pages of a very convenient size for use as wrappings for small articles such as cakes of soap, nailbrushes, and bottles of camomile and anti-midge lotion. It was in this capacity that Alison's eye had been caught while packing her suitcase for camp; and she now dropped on her knees and started searching feverishly through the papers and oddments that invariably collect in the bottom of suitcases. The doctor and the Inspector withdrew with the Professor and Armitage to the Professor's tent to continue their inquiries, leaving Alison to keep an eye on her husband, who was now sleeping quietly.

After frantic digging through torn and crumpled debris, Alison at last discovered the paper she sought. The short monograph entirely corroborated the knowledge which had been so tormenting her. Calling young Bertie Betts, she left him to keep a watch on the Colonel, and, armed with the paper, made her way to the Professor's tent. Inquiries were in full swing, the Professor looking pathetically worried, and Armitage more Mephistophelean than ever with his brows drawn down in a frown of anxiety.

"I think I can tell what the poison was," said Alison, advancing into the tent, paper in hand.

Doctor Hannaford looked up. "That would indeed be information worth having, my dear young lady," he replied with heavy sarcasm. "May I inquire how you come to be in possession of such vital information, which is outside the experience of the medical profession?"

The Inspector was less offensive, but equally incredulous. "If we knew the nature of the drug," he said, "we should be more than halfway towards finding the criminal; but the poison used in this case is one which has never before been recorded to our knowledge."

Alison appeared quite unmoved by this reception, though the Professor and Armitage recognised her resentment by the precise and somewhat clipped tones of her voice as she replied, "Judging by the symptoms, the drug would appear to be an obscure German synthetic, specially prepared for secret distribution among the higher war criminals, for use in the event of their being captured and brought to trial. In the majority of cases the dose is fatal within five minutes, but one or two cases have been known in which the constitution of the individual has been strong enough to withstand the first reaction, and once the first five minutes is withstood the victim exhibits symptoms exactly similar to those exhibited by my husband, and usually recovers within a few days." The group of men stared at Alison in amazement.

Then Dr. Hannaford recovered himself and, adjusting his horn-rimmed spectacles, regarded her with a bland smile. "That is certainly very interesting my dear Mrs. Enderby," he replied in a tone of kindly toleration, "but perhaps an expert such as yourself would be good enough in the first place to vouchsafe to us the source of your information, and in the second place to explain how such a substance as that which you mention would have escaped the notice of a mere amateur such as myself."

Alison laid the sheet of paper on the table. "It is all described here," she said shortly. "I don't see that you can require any more authentic source of information than that," pointing to the name of the publication at the top of the paper, "though how it has escaped your notice you should know better than I."

The doctor and the Inspector read the article closely, Armitage and the Professor leaning over their shoulders and following every word.

"Hmm," said Dr. Hannaford, somewhat nonplussed but fighting hard. "That would seem to be authentic enough. But," he went on, tapping the last paragraph of the article with a certain triumph in his manner, "I am afraid that somewhat nullifies your ingenious theory." The paragraph in question reads: "This drug has so far only been produced in extremely small quantities. As far as is known the individual capsules each containing the lethal dose have been issued, under conditions of extreme secrecy to the persons for whom they were intended, direct from the laboratory. It has never been produced commercially, and in fact is almost unknown outside a very restricted circle of German scientists."

"That would seem to put paid to your clever idea, I fear," said the doctor, whose professional pride had been stung by Alison's self-possessed attitude. "No, we must look elsewhere for the cause of your husband's seizure. I grant you that the symptoms appear to correspond, but in view of this statement I do not see the least possibility of this drug being the cause of the trouble."

The blandly patronising voice, and the 'don't be silly, little girl' manner, infuriated Alison almost beyond control. The Professor and Armitage, who knew something of her explosive temper, looked on apprehensively. Seeing the distress in her friends' faces Alison, though white with anger, managed to speak with a certain amount of restraint. She was obviously quite unaware of the enormity she was perpetrating in thus pitting her opinion against that of the famous criminologist.

"I shall make no attempt to influence your outlook, or the course of your investigations," she said sweetly, "but I shall continue my researches along my own lines, and if, as I fully anticipate, I find the criminal before you do, I hope that you will concede me the congratulations that I shall deserve." And with a charming smile, she withdrew, leaving the men speechless.

The Inspector found his voice first. “Well, I will be damned,” he exclaimed, “who does she think she is coming here trying to put it across us like that? Does she think she owns Scotland Yard, or what?”
Armitage laughed. “I don’t know about Scotland Yard,” he replied, “but I do know that she owns a better brain than most of us in this camp, and we are supposed to be a pretty bright lot in our way. I've even known her put one across the Professor before now.”
The Professor nodded agreement. “She is a very exceptional young lady, and of most deceptive appearance,” he said. “She carries a better brain and more acute perceptions behind that innocent face than anyone would credit.”
Inquiries and investigations went on rigorously and ruthlessly.
The Inspector and his assistants became a permanent part of camp life, and each and every member of the dig was questioned with a thoroughness that left them with the sensation of having been turned inside out and placed under a microscope. At the Professor’s earnest request the work at the excavations was allowed to go on, but no one was permitted to leave the camp and the excavators had to work under the eye of a constable.
“Might as well be a party of convicts on Dartmoor,” observed Armitage gloomily.
The presence of the police in camp was strongly resented at first, but the Inspector was a tactful soul, and when it was explained to the workers that their presence was a regrettable necessity owing to the suspected existence of a would-be murderer in their midst, the entire party swelled

with self-importance, and took the constabulary to their hearts without more ado. Amateur detectives sprang up like mushrooms and the whole camp revelled in a delightful orgy of sleuths, clues, and mystery.

The English students and workers were very soon cleared. The Professor could personally vouch for the great majority, and the others had unimpeachable credentials. The foreign students presented a rather different problem. One of the chief difficulties in the case was the entire lack of discoverable motive. Why anyone should wish to poison the quiet, efficient and popular Colonel, constituted one of the main problems. For poisoned he had certainly been, and by the use of an extremely rare drug, as Dr. Hannaford had at last been compelled to admit, which drug could only have been obtained by someone acquainted with pharmacy and having entry to a pharmaceutical laboratory. The only person who in any way fulfilled these requirements was Mrs. Enderby, and she was put through a gruelling examination which she survived with complete self-possession, somehow contriving to leave her questioners with the feeling that they were a party of rather foolish amateurs being kindly humoured by an expert.

Alison's challenge to Dr. Hannaford that she would find the criminal before he did, rapidly became known throughout the camp, and partisanship ran high. Armitage and Wilkinson ranged themselves at the head of her supporters, while the more cautious and less rashly chivalrous Baxter and Hardcastle rather apologetically sided with orthodox investigation. Feelings became acute, bets were freely laid, the junior members of the camp flung themselves joyously into the fray, and young Bertie Betts covered himself with blood and glory by punching and being punched by a senior high school boy, who had dared to cast aspersions on Bertie's heroine.

Some days elapsed before the credentials of the foreign students could be established, but, eventually all were satisfactorily checked up, each one being vouched for by the Principal of his own College or University.

This seemed to bring the investigations to a dead end; there appeared to be no-one in the entire party on whom suspicion could be placed. No-one could be found harbouring any grudge against the Colonel, nor could anyone, except Mrs Enderby be found who had any knowledge whatever of drugs or chemicals. It was all very disheartening, particularly to Dr. Hannaford, who, well aware of the partisan atmosphere throughout the camp, felt that his professional reputation was at stake.

In the middle of this stalemate attention was suddenly focussed on Mrs. Enderby, and this in the most unexpected way. To the dismay of her friends and adherents she began flirting and carrying on with the students in a way entirely foreign to her usual attitude of rather aloof toleration. The Professor and the old gang were dismayed beyond words. Man-like, they had placed her on a very high pedestal in their esteem and this unexplained departure from precedent left them shocked and hurt to the very core. Enderby himself was still too unwell to join in any of the activities of the camp and spent most of his time recuperating in a deckchair outside his tent. His meals were conveyed to him there, so he saw and knew nothing of the fresh developments, and none of his friends felt competent to tell him.

In the laughing circle which Alison collected round her it might have been noticed that the foreign students were always well to the fore; she seemed to avoid her own friends and to encourage all those that Armitage wrathfully described as “outsiders”.

Things came to a head one evening when Alison collected a party round her at dinner, and the proceedings at her end of the tent became absolutely riotous. The Professor was miserably distressed and bewildered. It was strange enough that she should desert her own seat at his side, a position which was hers by old established precedent, but that she should elect to gather a rowdy crowd in a far corner of the marquee, was really carrying things a bit too far. After dinner the old gang gathered disconsolately in the Professor’s tent, almost too distressed and dismayed for words.

Armitage, loyal as ever, spoke first. “I don’t care what anybody says,” he observed with a certain gloomy defiance, though no-one had opened his lips. “She’s playing some game of her own which is too deep for any of us to fathom as yet.”

“It is most undignified behaviour for one in her position, and a married woman too.” piped up little Baxter in virtuous tones.

“I can't think what’s possessing her,” said Hardcastle, “letting us all down like that.”

“Oh, shut up,” exclaimed Wilkinson. “I agree with Armitage. She is probably playing some deep game of her own, and in any case, no-one is going to make any derogatory remarks about her while I am around," and he glared so belligerently at the company that they all subsided without a further sound. An ex-P.T. instructor is not a safe person to argue with.

Dr. Hannaford and the Inspector had joined the group; in fact during the course of the investigations they had become quite a part of the camp, and very good friends with the Professor and the old gang. Only between Dr. Hannaford and Mrs. Enderby was there an atmosphere of armed neutrality. He, coming slowly to realise that she was a more formidable opponent than her youthfulness and innocent face would lead one to suppose, she, always perfectly gentle and polite, though treating him with a mocking sweetness in which there was more than a trace of patronage.

This sudden alteration in Alison's behaviour towards the students roused Dr. Hannaford's suspicions, for he had come to respect her far more than he would admit.

"I am inclined to think that Armitage and Wilkinson are right," he said. "She is certainly behaving in a very peculiar way, and quite unlike her usual manner I should imagine. She was playing some rowdy game with the foreign students at dinner time which seemed to centre round a bottle of Worcester sauce as far as I could see."

"She was apparently teaching them to call it Worcester and not Wor-ces-tor-shire," said the Professor unhappily, "though why she should need to encourage so much noisiness I cannot understand."

At that moment the tent flap was unceremoniously flung back, and Alison stepped into the lamp-lit circle. Her usually pale face was flushed, and there was something like defiance in her eyes as she gazed round the group. All the men immediately looked extremely sheepish, except Dr. Hannaford, who watched her keenly from behind his horn-rims.

"I have found the Criminal," she announced with well-simulated nonchalance, addressing herself to the Inspector and ignoring Dr. Hannaford entirely. "Get that student who calls himself a Dane and says his name is Gunnar Jensen and grill him a bit. I think you will find I am right."

Armitage let out a whoop of delight and drew Alison down on to the packing case beside him. "Good girl!" he exulted, treating her to a brotherly hug. "I knew you would do it. Come and tell us all about it."

The Inspector and Dr. Hannaford were out of their seats like a streak, but Alison called them back. "Ask him where he got his pharmaceutical experience," she said. "That will shake him, and the rest should be easy."

Despite the congratulations and delight of her friends Alison firmly refused to divulge anything. "If I am right I will tell you all about it," she said, "but I would rather wait till the Inspector has made his inquiries. Besides I want to see Dr. Hannaford's face," she added with an impish grin.

At the end of about an hour the Inspector and Dr. Hannaford returned to the tent, the former beaming with satisfaction and the latter eyeing Alison with a certain wariness.

"Well, we've got him," exclaimed the Inspector, rubbing his hands. "It is a most extraordinary story, and if it had not been for Mrs. Enderby spotting the right man by some method of her own, it would probably have had to be filed among the unsolved mysteries."

"Tell us the story," cried half a dozen voices, and the Inspector willingly obliged.

"It seems that this fellow is actually a German of the name of Friedrich von Winkelhausen," he said. "His father was one of the top-secret criminals that Colonel Enderby was instrumental in bringing to justice. This chap had been employed in the laboratories where this special drug was prepared and had been the chief agent entrusted to smuggle the capsules to the prisoners. His father was one of the rare cases, similar to Colonel Enderby, that resists the action of the drug, and he was eventually executed among the other war criminals. The son swore to avenge himself on the man that had compassed his father's death. He made his way to Denmark – where incidentally he had lived for many years and knew the language like a native – entered the University, which he knew frequently sent students to England, and, having provided himself with a couple of capsules saved from the demolition of the laboratory, he eventually tracked the Colonel down. We found another capsule concealed in the top of his fountain pen, and he was waiting till the Colonel returned to normal camp life in order to give him this second dose, which would certainly have been fatal. The drug is a tasteless powder which he had contrived to scatter over the Colonel's dinner while taking his turn as camp Orderly, to hand the plates round."

"It is all extremely satisfactory as far as that is concerned," said Dr. Hannaford, "but the question still remains – how did Mrs. Enderby spot the criminal?"

Alison picked up a bottle of calamine lotion from the packing case which served as the Professor's dressing table. She handed it to the Professor, and amid a staring and breathless silence, "Give that a shake and take the cork out," she said.

He shook the bottle to and fro in a rather gingerly manner, then carefully pulled the cork out between finger and thumb looking as if he thought it might explode at any moment. Alison smiled, took the bottle from him, and drove the cork home with the open-handed smack of long experience. Her eyes sought and held Dr. Hannaford's. "Now look," she said.

Gripping the bottle, she clamped her forefinger on the cork, turned the bottle upside down and shook it up and down with a vicious purposefulness. Then grasping the cork in the crook of the left little finger she pulled it out with a quick twist. Her audience stared uncomprehendingly, as if it had been a conjuring trick.

"What has all that got to do with finding the criminal?" asked Hardcastle at length.

Alison threw him a pitying glance, then looked at Dr. Hannaford again. "Do you follow me, doctor?" she asked, "or do I have to explain in words of one syllable?"

"My dear young lady," he replied, and there was deep and genuine admiration in his voice, "if I follow you correctly it is the prettiest bit of observation and deduction that I have come across in the course of a long and widely variegated career. But for the sake of our lay brethren I think you had better explain in – as you say – words of one syllable."

Alison looked round on the completely mystified group. "I was convinced," she said, "that Doc had been poisoned by the use of that particular drug when I recognised the characteristic pulse rhythm, of which I had read in that article. It is quite unmistakable, and was very clearly described, and no other condition gives that particular heart reaction. I also realised that the drug could only come into the possession of someone who had the entry to a pharmaceutical laboratory, and who understood something about chemistry and drugs. So, I took a long chance. I encouraged all those foreign students as it occurred to me that if anyone had a grudge against Doc it would probably be connected with his work on the War Crimes Commission. In other words, it boiled down to this – if I could find one of those foreigners who knew anything about pharmacy I would bet everything I possess that he was the man. That is why I got them all fooling round with that Worcester Sauce bottle."

Dr. Hannaford nodded delightedly, but every other face in the group remained blankly mystified. Alison looked round with slightly exasperated patience.

"You will have to put it in words of one syllable," said the doctor, "remember we are of the inner circle and they aren't."

"Well," she said, "shaking a bottle and taking out the cork is an infallible guide as to whether a person is in any way acquainted with the use of drugs. The average person handles them as the Professor did, very tenderly, and as if they might bite. Anyone who has had anything to do with chemistry or pharmacy grabs the bottle and shakes it as I did and hitches out the cork with the left little finger. Our pseudo-Danish friend was the only one who handled the Worcester sauce bottle in that way."

This story is based on a real-life scenario of an archaeological camp in the 1930's, before the outbreak of World War II. However, the poisoning of Colonel Enderby is fictitious.

Alison Enderby is based on Frances Roper and Colonel Enderby, is Doc Roper.

Doc and Nan (as she was called in those days) were both keen archaeologists, joining all sorts of excavations in West Sussex.

Major Arthur Cecil Roper (Doc) outside his tent on an archaeological dig in the 1960's, somewhere near the South Downs, Sussex.

38454629R00117

Made in the USA
Middletown, DE
08 March 2019